IDEAPRESS
PUBLISHING

IDEAPRESS
PUBLISHING

Published in the United States by IdeaPress Publishing,
an imprint of the Influential Marketing Group.

IDEAPRESS PUBLISHING

WE PUBLISH NON-OBVIOUS BUSINESS BOOKS

www.ideapresspublishing.com

All trademarks are the property of their respective companies.

Cover/Interior Design by Erin Tyler

Cataloging-in-Publication Data is on file with the Library of Congress.

ISBN: 978-1-940858-08-1

PRINTED IN THE UNITED STATES OF AMERICA

SPECIAL SALES

IdeaPress Books are available at a special discount for bulk purchases for
sales promotions and premiums, or for use in corporate training programs. Special
editions, including personalized covers, custom Forewards, corporate imprints and
custom bonus content are also available.

*No animals were harmed in the writing, printing or distribution of this book.
The trees, unfortunately, were not so lucky.*

NETWORKING
IS NOT
WORKING

STOP COLLECTING BUSINESS CARDS AND
START MAKING MEANINGFUL CONNECTIONS

DEREK COBURN

TABLE OF CONTENTS

FOREWORD

BY CHRIS BROGAN

Publisher of *Owner Magazine* and *New York Times* bestselling author

ON MEETING A PRINCE

ON MEETING A PRINCE

I'm unemployable. At this stage in my life, I've run a few companies and consulted with a lot of larger ones. There's really no hope for me in ever asking for a real job ever again. You know, a grown-up job.

My business is 100% based on networks. If I didn't have a network of friends and colleagues out there doing amazing work, I wouldn't know how to make a living. I thrive because of this and only this. Like a shark swimming, if I'm not moving, I will die. I exist purely because of the network.

For that reason, I have become very picky about networking: whether it's books or events. I've read many very bad books and been to thousands of bad events. Now I try to avoid them all. But then there is Derek Coburn.

Derek brought me to one of his events once. The differences were like night and day, like swimming and standing still:

* Derek brought me business. He paid for a bunch of my books in exchange for my time at the event (first win).

* He introduced me with great detail to his network of very caring and growth-minded colleagues (second win).

* They, in turn, bought a lot of my courses and into several of my projects over time (third win).

* I'm on Derek's very private Christmas mix CD mailing list (fourth win).

* I've had Derek speak at some of my events (fifth win).

* I've had the pleasure of talking with Derek's wonderful wife, Melanie, and seeing his family through Instagram (sixth win). And so on.

The difference between a master networker and someone who knows how to swap business cards is this: more wins. Derek continues to deliver endless value. It is his #1 goal. You could say it is his only goal. I could keep going. He introduced me to his chiropractor/sports medicine friend Dr. Jay Greenstein, who helped me via Skype once (seventh win). See? I could just keep doing this.

That's what you want. You want to learn how to network for life, for a thriving and endless relationship. This experience, this choice, this opportunity, is to become a prince of the city, the way Derek is in DC and beyond. The win is to become royalty and to have earned it.

This book, *Networking Is Not Working*, is an extension of everything Derek brings to his business relationships and to the world. It is filled with wins, with endless value, with lessons on networking for life.

My fear? That few people will dig in enough, will use the book the way it's intended, will realize the heart parts of this book are more important than the technical details. Use this book. Thrive within its covers, and then practice it. Live it.

That way, you'll network with me in a much more useful way, and I'll continue to swim. Seems like a fair deal. Agree?

CHRIS BROGAN

Publisher of Owner Magazine and
New York Times bestselling author

INTRODUCTION

INTRODUCTION

It was 11:30 on a Thursday night. I had just returned home from my second networking event of the week and I was exhausted. Once again, I had invested more than five hours of my time without much to show for it. It would have been nice to crash into my bed at that moment, but that wasn't an option. I had several client emails to respond to.

It was 2008 and we were in the early stages of what would turn out to be the worst economic crisis since the Great Depression. I owned a wealth management firm and my clients' portfolios were at the mercy of the stock market, which would eventually go down by 40%. They needed me more than ever.

At the same time, I needed to bring on new clients to offset my declining revenue. My income was directly tied to the value of my clients' portfolios. While we were doing better than most firms, losing 20%-30% of revenue definitely hurt, especially when I still had rent to pay, people to employ and mouths to feed. And those expenses didn't have the common courtesy to decline along with my revenue, which made writing checks that much more difficult.

At that point, I had built up a pretty good client base, which I mainly attribute to working 80 hours per week for 10 years. It was a long and draining process, particularly in the early years when I was a cold-calling machine. As my roster of clients expanded, however, I needed to find a more efficient way to meet new people.

Like most professionals, I thought the best way to grow my business was to network. And the primary way to do that was to attend networking events. Even though I viewed these events as a way to grow my client base, I was not expecting them to pay immediate dividends. I had a long-term approach. I wasn't under the illusion that I was instantly going to meet people who'd say "Oh my God! I came here because I wanted to meet a financial advisor. How do I give you all my money right this second?!"

I did have the reasonable expectation, I thought, that I was going to meet and connect with other professionals in a meaningful way and, eventually, welcome some amazing new clients to my practice. Unfortunately, this was an expectation that rarely realized itself. Why wasn't every-thing in the books and all the advice I had ever heard on networking...working? I was constantly taking business cards and bouncing from client meetings to networking events. I was doing everything they talked about, and it wasn't like I was expecting to hold the world in my hands. What was I doing wrong?

It wasn't until I had to start devoting extra time to my clients, which left me with even less time to network, that I realized my approach had never been an effective one.

It turns out the odds of yielding rewarding, long-term pro-fessional relationships vs. the time I was allocating toward this goal were poor, at best. Worse, I couldn't keep this up without sacrificing time I would otherwise spend focusing on my existing clients; time I could ill-afford to lose.

The direness of my situation was a blessing in disguise. It forced me to revisit the over-arching goals I had for my busi-ness: to provide a great experience for my existing clients, while adding more of them to my practice. It became clear to me that if I wanted to do that, I needed to do something completely different. So, I started to identify more effective ways to accomplish my goals. I left no stone unturned, no avenue unexplored, no sacred cow un-slaughtered.

What follows is an outline of the unconventional networking strategies that emerged from this process. Collectively, these strategies grew my revenue by over 300% in just 18 months. Not surprisingly, large, traditional networking events were not part of this picture. The cornerstone of these strategies is something I call "un-networking." I will lay out for you the steps I took to create this unique, counterintuitive version of a "networking group"[1] for myself. Consisting of approximately 25 handpicked professionals, its limited, curated nature allowed me to facilitate valuable connections and create opportunities for the people in my network. Finally, I will show you how to turn the value you create for these group members into more ideal clients for your own business.

These strategies make up the core of this book.

---

1   In my case, the success derived from this intimate group led to the creation of an "un-networking" community in Washington, DC called cadre, which I co-founded with my wife Melanie. As of this writing, that community has 100+ CEOs and business owners, who we serve as members, and has started expanding into other cities.

WHO THIS BOOK WILL HELP (AND WHO IT WON'T)

I'll be straight with you: unless you're open to the idea of kicking traditional networking to the curb and embracing a new perspective, this book is probably not for you. What I share in these pages will not be helpful if you are looking for:

1) Tips on how to use networking events to get direct, immediate business

2) A new job

There is nothing wrong with incorporating these goals into your approach to networking—it's just that I won't be offering up anything useful if either of these is your endgame.

What I will provide is an alternative to the time you may currently be spending on your networking efforts. I implemented most of what I will be sharing with you by eliminating the larger networking events, and using that time to focus on some unconventional strategies. The strategies in this book are designed to accomplish one of three things (sometimes all at once):

- Increasing the quantity and quality of value you provide your best clients

- Identifying and developing relationships with other remarkable and relevant professionals

- Positioning yourself to get more quality introductions to prospective ideal clients

After I began implementing these strategies, I was able to provide even more value for my existing clients. I became more efficient, and the quality of my clients, and my life, improved dramatically. I do believe that following my blueprint will allow many of you to experience the same type of growth that I achieved (including to the bottom line).

HOW TO USE THIS BOOK

Networking Is Not Working is (informally) organized into two parts. The first two chapters assess networking on a higher level—both why the traditional approach is flawed and how certain key experiences led to a shift in my approach to networking.

The second part of the book will provide a step-by-step guide for putting my unconventional networking strategies into action. Through a process that I call CONECTOR, I will provide the roadmap for becoming a connector and show how it will transform your business and life.

Most of what I will share about how to leverage the CONECTOR approach can be applied on a one-off basis. If you want to pick and choose what's workable for you, that's fine. However, I put all of the pieces together to form my own networking group based on my new definition of networking. If you are a super-connector who loves helping people and want to take full advantage of my approach, let this book be your guide.

CHAPTER 01

WHY TRADITIONAL NETWORKING IS NOT WORKING

WHY TRADITIONAL NETWORKING IS NOT WORKING

There are many reasons why networking is not working, but the most common source of frustration involves the role of networking events themselves. Large, traditional networking events are a time-honored institution. They have been a staple of aspiring professionals for so long that most networking advice centers not on *whether* you should attend them, but how to make the most of them when you inevitably do. In theory, they're one of the best ways to grow your business. After all, most advice will tell you that a networking event is a room full of people just like you (business professionals) looking for the same thing you are (clients and growth). It's fish in a barrel and everyone has a gun. The logic of this arrangement has become unimpeachable the larger these events get, to the point where large networking events have become sacred cows.

Here's the problem: you're almost certainly not getting
the consistent results you're looking for. And at some point,
when the majority of professionals taking part in these rituals
are seeing drastically diminished returns on their investment
in them, we have to start looking at networking itself.

If you asked 20 people who consider networking essential to their success what the word means to them, you'd
probably get 20 different answers: business development,
anxiety, finding a job, extroversion, necessary evil.

None of these descriptions is incorrect, but all of them
are different.

Here is the definition from Merriam-Webster: *the exchange
of information or services among individuals, groups,
or institutions; specifically the cultivation of productive
relationships for employment or business.*

Not bad, but still fairly broad. And I highly doubt that
would have been one of the responses you got from your
20-person sample.

In an effort to get us on the same page, I have come up
with a definition that I hope will resonate with you. It is the

definition I will be applying to the word "networking" every time I use it throughout this book.

NETWORKING: any activity that increases the value of your network and/or the value you contribute to it.

Regardless of how you define networking, your level of success will be directly tied to your ability to interact with other professionals who are looking to achieve many of the same things you are with your business. Unfortunately, this will be challenging if you rely on larger events because, like it or not, the deck is stacked against you.

NETWORKING EVENTS – THE NIGHTCLUBS OF BUSINESS DEVELOPMENT

The most basic problem with traditional networking events is that they are mixing bowls for professionals who are there for different reasons. No matter how you slice it, everyone in the room is focused on his or her own personal agenda, whether it be signing up a new client, creating awareness for their business, or connecting with someone in the hopes of developing a mutually beneficial relationship. It's an "every man/woman for themselves" kind of game, and since everyone is playing a slightly different game, there are usually no clear winners.

I was at an event once and a guy came up to me and introduced himself. Introductions are always tricky because everyone usually has a "strategy"—they have a go-to line or a quick elevator pitch. This guy breezed through his introduction like a normal person, then proceeded to talk about himself for no fewer than four straight minutes. Try listening to someone for four minutes straight who you have not paid to see speak. It's impossible, especially when you were expecting to have a conversation, which requires two people to take the time to actively and respectfully listen to each other. One minute into his spiel, it was obvious I was being pitched to, so I checked out. He wrapped up by giving me his card and walking away.

The majority of professionals who regularly attend networking events are not as bad as this but they suffer from the same problem: they are looking for instant gratification. And because they want success *now,* they use bad metrics such as new "potential" clients engaged, or number of meetings scheduled, to define that success and determine its magnitude.

In a recent article for the *Wall Street Journal*, Gary Vaynerchuk—the master networker and businessman— hammers this point home, reminding us that there are still many people "who think 'good networking' is predicated on the distribution of business cards; that giving a card to anybody in the room is somehow meaningful or useful." Gary V is right on the money when he says, "Effective networking is about reversing the game everybody instinctively plays. It's about patience and buildup, not the close. We celebrate audacity and courage instead of patience and value."

In my four-minute "interaction," Business Card Billy never took the time to ask for my name. He didn't have the patience to ask the name of my business. In fact, he didn't ask me anything at all. He was so focused on his reason for being at this event—telling anyone who will listen about his business—that he forgot about *me*. He reminded me of Bette Midler's character from *Beaches:* "Enough about me, let's talk about you. What do *you* think about me?"

The man's only saving grace was that he left before he could spill anything on me like so many of those other networking event attendees who like to wave their hands around while telling you how great they are. These guys almost always have a drink in their hand and some of it invariably ends up on your shirt. I don't want to think about how much I've spent on dry cleaning over the last decade just on drink-splattered shirts from networking events.

Needless to say, we've all experienced networking nightmares like this. Of course there will also be professionals at these events who, like you, have a long-term view and are looking to establish meaningful connections with other attendees. But they are becoming fewer and farther between.

Instead, you're getting people like Mr. Me Me Me, or folks

who show up looking for a job. I don't have a major issue with the job seekers. Getting out and meeting people is what they should be doing. Heck, their presence can even be beneficial: meeting someone who could be a great employee for someone else in your network can put you in the position of creating real value for your network as a whole if you connect them.

More often than not, however, conversations with job seekers do not lead anywhere. I get frustrated whenever I go to an event and end up meeting people whose only objective is securing my email so they can pass along their resume. This approach never works. If I am looking to hire a new employee, I know exactly what I need and I go out to find it. I do not leave it up to chance at large networking events. But here's the thing: from the email-securing jobseeker's perspective, our interaction was a success, even though (objectively speaking) meeting me was not good for either of us.

In many ways, including the ways I've just described, traditional networking is a lot like dating. It's a part of life you get more tired of the older you get, especially as it gets harder to find people who are looking for the same things you are. Networking events are the apotheosis of this problem. As David Siteman Garland, creator of The Rise To

The Top & Create Awesome Online Courses put it, "Networking events are like nightclubs, because most people there are just looking for a professional one-night stand."

As a businessperson, for your networking efforts to be successful, you need to be in a room full of your ideal prospective clients. This is obviously not the case with large networking events. So walking around acting like everyone could benefit from hiring you and eagerly telling them how great your business is does you no good. In fact, it can do you a fair amount of harm, since telling us how great your products and services are immediately after introducing yourself is, essentially, in-person cold calling—which everyone despises.

To expand on the dating analogy, books about finding your ideal partner or "soul mate" generally don't advise you to go to nightclubs every night. If you're looking to meet someone nice who might be suitable for a committed relationship, why would you waste your time in a crowded place that is so loud you can't even hear yourself think? Plus, it's not like you're going to meet many people who are there for the same reason you are. It's common sense. Everyone gets that!

Instead, the best dating books suggest that you leverage your friendships and expose yourself to environments that are more conducive to finding a compatible mate. Get personal introductions from friends, host dinner parties, let the people who know you best set you up. Dating for love is not a volume business. Networking for the long-term benefit of your business is the exact same thing, or at least it *should* be.

Unfortunately, all of the networking books and articles I have read focus their advice on how to make the most out of networking by *attending events.* It's as if there is only one game to play, and the key is to play that game a certain way. Namely, A LOT. The ritual of the large networking event, and the shared motivations of its players, is so firmly entrenched that I am dubious about its ability to accommodate new approaches. The good news, as you will see in later chapters, is that you don't actually have to play that game at all.

WATCH OUT FOR PROFESSIONAL ONE-NIGHT STANDS

If you're anything like me, you've spent many an evening at networking events trying to shake off the onslaught of professional one-night standers while searching for the professional equivalent of an ideal mate. Needless to say, we usually go home disappointed. Why is that? What is wrong with us?

Let me ask that question another way: If you were making more money than you ever imagined working with clients you absolutely loved and had more high-quality prospects looking to hire you than you had time for, how often would you go to networking events?

I am guessing your answer would be, "Hardly ever" or "Only if I had to."

Running a successful business leaves little time for networking. As the quality of your clients and the value of your business increase, so too will the value of your time.

Before long, you will find yourself jealously guarding that time not just for yourself, but also for your clients and the business you have taken such great pains to develop. It's only natural then that you will be less likely to subject yourself to large, cattle-call networking events.

It is for these very reasons that you will rarely find your ideal professional mate at a networking event. These are also the reasons why the *regular* attendees at networking events are almost always one-night standers. They are the people who are just starting out or running a flailing, mediocre business and looking for anyone who might be able to help (or save) them in any way. They are looking for quick fixes, short-term remedies, stop-gap measures. They aren't worried (yet) about cultivating long-term relationships, so fittingly they have the most time to spare on networking. I do not fault them necessarily. It's hard to focus on developing long-term relationships when you have to worry about paying the mortgage next month or making payroll next week. However, that doesn't mean we have to be their next victims.

I'm sorry to be the one to break the bad news and burst the networking bubble, but the fact remains that professionals trying to get something out of you, whose product or service is too unremarkable to yield new clients in a more efficient manner, represent the majority of attendees at networking events. The people you *really* want to meet are busy making better use of their time. This dichotomy is what makes most of us dread showing up to events.

And yet, we still go. It's been drilled into us that the only way to find diamonds is to forage in this rough. This is how my relationship with networking morphed until my growing client base—and the time I needed to devote to it—made me question the hours I spent in said rough and forced me to reevaluate my strategy for finding diamonds. In reality, I should have seen it coming, as it was eerily similar to the inflection point I arrived at during my early cold-calling days. Hopefully, I can save you the thousands of hours I wasted by shining a spotlight on the inefficiencies of attending these larger events.

NETWORKING EVENTS VS. COLD-CALLING

In the early years of growing my practice, I did not have a lot of existing clients to take care of and spent just about every waking hour either in meetings, or trying to set them up.

I knew if I called 300 people every day, 30 would let me talk to them and six would schedule a meeting. Of those six, one would become a client. Getting new clients and growing my business was the only thing that mattered, so I was unconcerned with the fact that it took 6-10 hours of constant effort to yield one client; let alone that my conversion rate was .003%, or 1/3 of one percent.

I was also not concerned whether my new client would be a *good* client. If someone wanted to work with me, I was happy to have them. The fact that I needed them more than they needed me—or at least that's what I let myself think—led me to spend a lot of time spinning my wheels, trying to please them. For many of these clients, I was fighting a losing battle, because what I could provide was not exactly what they were looking for. It was like the dance of the square peg and the round hole.

I don't blame my old clients, though. I had contacted them out of the blue and they didn't really know much about me. There wasn't much chance our working relationships would be long and fruitful. As those engagements began to fade away, the reality of my business became much clearer. I didn't want or need (nor could I afford) clients just for the sake of clients. I needed to find my *ideal* clients. The good news is, after a few years, I had developed a solid group with whom I enjoyed working. The bad news, at least in retrospect, was that it took way more than 6-10 hours to find each of them. When you factor in all the extra work I did to engage and service those clients who were not a good fit, it took *days* of constant effort to find one who was.

This was not a tenable situation. Nor was it scalable. There was no way I could grow if this is how it was going to be. Getting a taste of these more rewarding client experiences drove that point home and made me begin to value my time more. It gave me the confidence to do away with smiling and dialing.

My clients were happy about it too, even if they weren't aware of my shift in perspective, because I was now spending more time focusing on their needs. Not surprisingly, I began getting great referrals from some of them. The people on the other end of these introductions were obviously much easier to engage than the folks I was cold-calling. Like dating, you're more likely to hit it off when a mutual friend sets you up than you are going down the row hitting on strangers at the club.

Still, when I finally made the shift, I was not busting at the seams with ideal clients who were keeping me busy 100% of the time. I needed to dedicate *some* time towards growing my business. It was at this point that I started focusing even more on networking events and attending them more frequently. I enjoyed them for the most part and convinced myself for several years that they were a good use of my time. They were face-to-face, after all, and everyone in attendance had chosen to be there. Networking events were light years away from the intrusive drudgery of cold-calling. That's what I told myself anyway.

Part of the reason I fooled myself into believing I was spending my time wisely was because I was comparing networking events to cold-calling. Cold-calling is a business development practice that is nowhere near as prevalent as it once was. Today, most people have cell phones with Caller ID and have put their phone numbers on federal "Do Not Call" lists. This makes just getting through to someone a nearly impossible task and compels many newcomers to skip over what so many of us had to endure in favor of going straight to networking.

If you've never had to cold-call as a way to develop new business, you have been spared the brutal, non-stop agony of rejection. Unlike cold-calling or following up on dead-end leads, with networking events there is no fear of (or actual experience of) rejection. There is only a harmless exchange of business cards or email addresses followed by empty promises to "connect" or "circle back" later in the week. Doesn't the removal of immediate rejection auto-matically make networking events better than cold-calling?

I now know, based on my experience and regular atten-dance, that the answer is No. Networking events aren't any more productive—or less intrusive—than cold-calling. Your chances of meeting someone who aligns with your goals are no better face-to-face with a perfect stranger than they are over the phone with someone who isn't expecting your call. And at least with immediate rejection you save valuable time.

Don't worry, I am not about to advocate cold-calling as an alternative to attending networking events! What I'm sug-gesting is that we have a tendency to think we are being productive while networking because there is no negative reinforcement when it's not working. My fear is that many professionals are wasting the same amount of time, and without the fear of rejection driving them to escape this time-suck, it will continue until there is no time left and their businesses have failed.

By the same token, I am also not saying you should abandon networking as a practice. Networking, whether online or off, can be a great way to grow your business and add value to your network. The problems come from *how* you do it. You must have a defined approach. Just doing it, just showing up, will never consistently lead you to the types of professionals with whom long-term business relationships are possible, let alone profitable.

Don't get me wrong, it can work from time to time. Despite some of the more extreme examples I just laid out, most of your interactions at networking events are with nice people who make for seemingly harmless conversations. And once in a while, those conversations are with great people who actually appear to share your worldview. Unfortunately, many of them will present their own set of challenges.

TOO GOOD TO BE TRUE?

Of late, a more evolved form of networking—let's call it Networking 2.0—has arisen from a bevy of advice books. Taking a page from John F. Kennedy's 1961 Inaugural Address ("Ask not what your country can do for you…"), they tell us to focus not on what other people at networking events can do for us, but what we can do for them.

Can we introduce them to someone? Do we have a piece of unsolicited strategic advice we could give them? Maybe we could refer them to prospective clients?

I am all for this shift in focus, in theory. I love connecting people. And plenty of professionals with good intentions, who are not looking to pitch their business (i.e. the ones you want to meet), still go to networking events, so it could absolutely work. Plus, my way of thinking and my long-term view on developing professional relationships already comport with most of the advice these kinds of books offer up.

Here's the problem though: much of the Networking 1.0 crowd (Mr. Me Me Me, for instance) read these books too, and realized that if they showed just a modicum of interest in the person they were meeting—they didn't need to actually be interested—it could lead to more business. It would take a little longer, sure, but if they put forth even a little effort—the minimum amount—other professionals would feel obligated to do the same for them, only better.

Almost immediately, the new philosophy that could have saved networking events made them more difficult. The people who made them miserable to attend, who we tried to avoid at all costs, became harder to spot. They blended right in with the real professionals we value so highly. Now if I'm at a networking event and someone wants to learn more about me and how they can help me, all it does is set off my bullshit detector. My first thought is "what's the catch?" They could be sincere, I know, but it's more likely they're taking this tack because they read about it in a book. I'm sure many of you have already discovered this for yourselves in the world of networking: those people asking how they can help you right off the bat are not interested in helping you. They're interested in you helping them.

I learned this lesson the hard way. As someone who initially embraced the Networking 2.0 approach, I was all for indiscriminately "paying it forward." I would help anyone and everyone I encountered. A reference, an email address, advice, a tip, it didn't really matter what they needed, because it was all going to come back around to me in the end, like business karma. And boy did it ever.

At one point, I introduced a new acquaintance from a recent event to a very good client of mine. This new connection appeared to be a good guy with a good business, so making the introduction seemed likely to create some potential synergies. I connected them via email with a nice, complimentary note and let them take it from there to set up a call or a lunch or whatever would work for their purposes.

The day after their first meeting, my client called. My new acquaintance had pitched him within the first 20 minutes. It was horrible, and his pitch was worse. My client had called to warn me about him more than anything, but I'm sure he was questioning my judgment at least a little bit. Fortunately their encounter didn't ruin my existing business relationship, but lesson learned:

> **NEVER** put your reputation on the line with clients by introducing them to people you don't know much about.

Think about it: why should you go out of our way to advance the business interests of someone you just met, when it means involving someone whose business interests you are already being paid to protect and advance? It is a recipe for disaster.

This brings me to another dating analogy. Let's say Mary is out on the town one evening with her girlfriends and a seemingly nice guy named Gary strikes up a conversation with her. Now, Mary is interested in having a committed relationship, but she's *at a bar* to dance and hang out with her friends—not to find a soul mate. What would her reaction be if, shortly after exchanging pleasantries, Gary tells Mary that he's looking to settle down and get married? She'll either 1) assume he's hitting on her and masking his true intentions or 2) think he's serious...which is kind of worse. (Psycho alert!)

As much as she might want a relationship, Mary will not react favorably to Gary's advances. Making this kind of declaration to someone you just met at a bar is not consistent with the expectations in this environment. When you're sitting on a barstool it comes off as creepy. When you're at a networking event, it comes off as bullshit.

Don't believe me? Just for fun, the next time you attend a networking event, strike up a conversation with someone and immediately tell them you're looking to develop a meaningful professional relationship, and you'd like to know how you can help them. What do you guess their reaction is going to be? Actually, you don't have to guess because I've already tested this on more than one occasion. It went about as well as our friend Gary's unsolicited pronouncements of monogamy and matrimonial intent. Which is to say, it went really bad.

A pay-it-forward approach is not without merits. It should just be reserved for professionals you know and have confidence in. If you focus on helping someone you don't know in order to start a *quid pro quo* game for your own benefit, you run the risk of putting someone you *do* know in the hands of someone who will waste their time or worse, take advantage of them. How will that make you look?

In the words of Warren Buffett, "It takes a lifetime to build a reputation and only 15 minutes to destroy it."

FINALLY! BUT, ALAS…

As I worked my way through the evolution of networking, one of the keys I figured out was strategically identifying people you can help who can also help you. This is a skill in and of itself, but even those of us who got good at it could run into some really frustrating situations. I cannot even begin to count the number of times I've met a promising business contact only to run smack into another pitfall of traditional networking: Email Purgatory.

I had a process for following up with worthy folks I met through various networking channels. Within a day or two of meeting, I'd look at their websites and scour their LinkedIn profiles to get a better sense of who they were and how we might be able to collaborate. Then I'd email them to express my earnest desire to continue exploring whether we could help each other. I wouldn't ask for a meeting. Like our face time at the event where we met, my communication was not "sales-y." I practiced Networking 2.0 to the letter.

And yet, what kind of response did I get? Not much. There were times when I'd email someone after a seriously great introduction and my helping hand was completely ignored. *Really?* I'd think, *You don't have time to respond to someone who could be a great source of potential referrals?* If you were to ask those people today why they didn't reply back then, I'd be willing to bet it had nothing to do with the medium or the message. It wasn't because I was a jerk or spamming the hell out of them. There was something else going on.

The problem, I realized soon enough, was dedicated time. Responding to emails takes time, and time is money.

That's why the post-event email routine is fundamentally flawed. Unconsciously, you are assuming your counterpart is exactly as busy and just as eager to connect as you are. But there is just so much happening on the other end you couldn't possibly know about, that it's foolhardy to have any kind of expectations. You never know what someone else might be going through. Your contact could simply have something more pressing going on that day: a family issue, a client issue, or something revenue-generating. If they don't have the bandwidth the day you email or they aren't in the mood to start developing a new business relationship that week, it's not going to happen.

Slowly but surely, I came to the conclusion that networking events weren't any better than cold-calling; in fact, they were probably worse. In the beginning I didn't think either one was all that bad. For a while I actually liked going to networking events. The difference was that now, unlike when I was first starting out, I had a business to run and clients to take care of. I started noticing how much time all of this networking was taking, and how little return I was getting on my investment.

For a glimpse into the time-sucking world, consider these time expenditures:

- Attending networking events, actively meeting and mingling

- Sifting through people—names, faces, companies, titles, personal details, etc.

- Identifying and researching contacts who might have potential as clients or partners

- Crafting and sending emails to these contacts

- Having lunch, coffee, etc. with those you hit it off with

Let's assume you're great at each of these things and you complete them with the utmost efficiency. Conservatively, this is still at least 24 hours out of your week. That's a *full* day you've lost, a day that could have been used to service clients and contacts you already have. Over the course of a year, that's 50+ days. *Seven weeks!* Can you imagine what else you could do to grow your current business with seven weeks?

Now I am not suggesting that you never attend another networking event. They can be valuable if leveraged properly. What I am saying is, if you agree that networking is any activity that increases the value of your network and/or the value you contribute to it, there are a number of alternatives that will save you time and accelerate the growth of your business.

I am excited to share them with you in the pages to come.

CHAPTER 02

FROM NETWORKING TO UN-NETWORKING

FROM NETWORKING TO UN-NETWORKING

↻

In his excellent book, *UnMarketing*, Scott Stratten tells the story of a local networking event he attended where, in the space of a few minutes, a real estate agent exposed all the problems with traditional networking:

"...with card already in hand, [he] walked up to me and introduced himself, shoving his card at me. I replied with my name and asked why he was giving me his card. His reply was 'That's what we're here for, to exchange information, to network!'...I proceeded to then listen to him talk about his web site and how if we gave him our cards that he had a section where he would post a link to us and in return we could post one for him on ours! Taadaa! Sigh..."

In the process of relating this story, Stratten casually coined the term *UnNetworking* to suggest the need to unlearn not just the old ways of marketing, but the old ways of networking, and define a new approach that can consistently attract and engage the right customers and clients in the 21st century economy. It was a term that stuck with me and came to life one day, when I found myself involved in an interaction that would completely change the way I approached and defined networking.

One of my clients is a landscaper—let's call him David. David gets a call from one of his high-end clients, asking him to meet with a financial advisor he (the client) knows. "This guy is great," David's client said. "We know you have Derek and you like him, but you have to meet this guy. It would be a huge favor to me, regardless of whether anything comes of it." You know the persuasive words and pleading tone you get when someone really, *really* wants something from you? Well, this client laid it on thick.

David told me about the conversation. He said I had nothing to worry about, but that he felt obligated to take this meeting. Then he asked if I could give him the information on his accounts to share with this other guy. So I did. I wasn't particularly excited about it, but if I'd tried to withhold, I would have just pushed David into this guy's arms.

After his meeting, David called to share what went down. The financial advisor thought he had made a good, logical argument for why he could do what I did—only better. He outlined how David could have earned 3% more in his portfolio over the past two years, had he invested with him instead of me. End of story? I lost a client, right? Not even close.

David came back with this: "Derek has referred me two clients that have generated over $2 million in revenue for my business in the past two years. So in theory, he could have lost half the money in my portfolio, and from a net worth perspective, I would still have been better off working with him."

Driving the point home, he told the financial advisor, "Hypothetically, even if you would have been better than him at managing my investments, why would I leave a relationship with someone who is doing a great job *and* referring me business?"

THE ULTIMATE TIEBREAKER

David's words were an epiphany. Right there on the phone I had a moment of clarity: If I was already adding this kind of value to my clients' portfolios *and their businesses*, how much more could I create if I actually made it a priority by weaving it into my suite of services and bolstering my value proposition? At that moment, I realized I was on to something. I needed to enhance my efforts to make my clients and their businesses an even greater focal point of my business and networking efforts.

This new approach would prove to be more powerful than I ever imagined.

These days, most of us are in a commodity business, whether we like it or not. Globalization has leveled the playing field to the point where it's become increasingly difficult for anyone to say they're objectively better than their competitors. Is McDonald's better than Burger King? Is Apple better than Samsung? Maybe to some. But if one was clearly better—all the time and for everyone—the others would go out of business.

It takes more to stand out in this hyper-connected world than simply declaring yourself a standout. You have to actually *do* something to differentiate yourself, and you need to do it in a meaningful way, if you want to actually stand out from the competition. I now believe there is no better way to set yourself apart than to **refer clients to your clients and facilitate these valuable connections.** Of course I still needed to keep meeting or exceeding expectations as a financial advisor (you know, do my job), but by doing something valuable for my clients, namely getting them more clients, I could effectively eliminate my competition. Actively helping clients grow their bottom line is the Ultimate Tiebreaker.

> **IMPORTANT DISCLAIMER #1:** If you do **not** do great work and you do not already deliver a valuable service for your clients, adding this new kind of benefit will not matter.

> **IMPORTANT DISCLAIMER #2:** Do *not* make this kind of promise to a client (or prospect) unless you truly believe you can deliver. It's fine to have clients who are not elite in their fields; just don't set this kind of expectation for them. I recommend David because he is my client, but more importantly, because he is awesome and does amazing work. You

won't always be in a position to introduce someone to their ideal client. If you meet someone who only works with Fortune 100 companies and you don't have any relationships in that space, it would be inauthentic to suggest you can add this type of value.

In Jay Baer's recent bestseller, *Youtility: Why Smart Marketing Is About Help Not Hype*, he suggests, "What if instead of trying to be amazing you just focused on being useful? What if you decided to inform, rather than promote?" He continues, "Youtility is massively useful information, provided for free, that creates long-term trust and kinship between your company and your customers." By utilizing your network to refer clients to your clients, you make yourself an extension of their business development and marketing teams. Your value to them is now multi-faceted and you are simultaneously deepening your client's trust in you and expanding that trust into new arenas. This is how the Ultimate Tiebreaker works.

THE ULTIMATE RESOURCE

The Ultimate Tiebreaker was a revelation that had the potential to make me extremely valuable to my clients, particularly those who were responsible for bringing in new business. But what about my other clients? The C-Suite executives, HR directors, and law firm administrators? Some were personal financial planning clients, and others were corporate clients whose 401k and benefit plans my firm had established and served. They were not responsible for bringing in new business; *they were decision makers*. What they needed was a go-to resource for helping them make decisions. In that, I discovered another way I could leverage my network to add significant value for my clients: I would become the Ultimate Resource.

If you are world-class in your field, then you are providing major value to your clients just by plying your trade. That's good. At the transactional, client-vendor level, everyone wins. But an Ultimate Resource has the ability to go beyond the transactional. S/he can connect and provide a client with access to dozens of people who are world-class in other fields.

Here's an example: One of my clients had just vested on a large block of stock options and wanted to treat herself to her dream car. As her financial advisor, I encouraged her not to invest everything and to enjoy some of the fruits of her labor. Now, if you were in her shoes, how comfortable would you be negotiating the price of a six-figure car with some random car salesman?

Fortunately, she had me in her corner. I knew the best and most trustworthy car salesman in town: CC Sloan of Rosenthal Automotive. I had a great experience buying a car from him. Then he helped my wife find her car (despite the fact he did not carry the particular manufacturer she wanted). Because he went above and beyond to help her when it did not directly benefit him, I decided he was someone I could trust with my clients. They wouldn't have to subject themselves to a stressful (and potentially costly) car-buying process.

To make a long story short, my client got her dream car and was so thrilled with CC that she asked for his address to send him a bottle of wine. Do you know of anyone who has ever bought a thank-you gift for their car salesman? He made me look like a hero, and my client was very appreciative.

It's in instances like this where many of us have been

trained to expect something in return from the CC in this scenario. I gave him a referral, now he owes me right? Absolutely not! It doesn't matter because that's not why I did it. (You could even argue that I owed *him*.) Simply by being remarkable at what he does, he helped me further cement the relationships I had with my best clients.

By holding myself out as well-connected to all the top businesses in my orbit—the best contractor, the best realtor, the best chiropractor, the best car salesman—I made myself the go-to guy. I saved my clients time by making their decisions easier and, with each successful recommendation, further solidified their trust in me.

And of course, this added tremendous value for the companies I recommended. It came full circle. Once these vendors realized the value I could bring to them by making these introductions, it usually occurred to them that their current financial advisor wasn't doing this. I was generating business for myself without a single elevator pitch.

Now, as with the Ultimate Tiebreaker strategy, it cannot be stressed enough that for this to work, you need to identify and only recommend top-shelf businesses and people— not necessarily your clients or people who are referring business to you. Otherwise, not only will you fail at being the Ultimate Resource, but you could also harm your reputation and your business.

Some of you may be thinking "What if I don't have a large network of high-quality folks right now?" Don't worry. I have you covered. For now, just assume this reality as your own and think about how beneficial it will be for you down the road. But more importantly, do not enter into becoming an Ultimate Resource with the expectation of short-term returns.

Case in point: for a time there, one of the more frequent requests I got from clients was for an introduction to an estate-planning attorney. When you do your job well as a financial advisor, the end result is wealth, which your clients then have to figure out what to do with once they're gone. After meeting with many of the top attorneys in town, I identified the best one and started referring some of my best clients to her. She did a great job, but never referred any of her clients to me. There were other attorneys in town who were much more receptive to a quid-pro-quo relationship—and admittedly, that would have been better for me in the short term—but it didn't matter. I was not "giving to get." My intention was to be a resource and make my clients' lives easier. My goal was to increase the value I brought to my clients and to build up my reputation as their Ultimate Resource. This woman was the best person for the job, and that's all there was to it.

A SHIFT IN MINDSET

So why was I networking? It started with the desire to build my client base and generate more business. Then it graduated to wanting to replicate the mutually reward- ing relationships I had developed naturally. When I began using my connections to benefit my clients, with the intention of becoming more of a resource than a vendor or service provider, I discovered I could accomplish all of those things *in a more meaningful and lasting way*. I would now network in order to provide solutions and **add more value for my existing clients.**

I continued going to networking events, only now I wasn't thinking about myself or how my financial services could directly (or indirectly) help the people I was meeting. My focus shifted to learning about their issues and finding a solution—one that could leverage the considerable resources of the clients, partners and other people in my existing network and benefit everyone involved.

It went something like this: When I met someone at an event and introduced myself as a financial advisor, the typical response was "Oh....uh...I don't need a financial advisor right now because..." a) I already have a financial advisor; b) Insert any lame excuse/change of subject technique; or c) I'm saving my money to buy a new house right now.

That last option was gold. I could take that and run with it (assuming they were being honest and weren't just trying to blow me off). Knowing that they were in the market for a new home, I would offer up my help. I would respond with "I have a great real estate agent I can recommend," which gave me the opportunity to add value in several ways:

1) I can make a connection for a strategic partner of mine. In this case, a trusted real estate agent. This introduction could amount to something for him.

2) When I refer someone to a good real estate agent who ends up taking care of him, I was a resource. If they end up buying their dream house, I helped make that happen.

3) Taking a longer view, the sooner they buy the house, the sooner they'll be in a place to start investing their

money—hopefully with me, since I helped pave the way into that house.

Focusing on yourself (Networking 1.0) and claiming you're there to help the person you've just met by providing whatever product or service you have to offer (Networking 2.0) are both likely to put people on their guard. However, because most people are receptive to sharing their challenges and open to helpful suggestions, this new approach—Networking 3.0—is much more effective.

I knew I was onto something, but I wasn't quite there yet. For one thing, I was only half the equation. Most people at large networking events were focused only on pitching their products and services. They were not looking for help, so my solution-oriented strategy wasn't working. It wasn't even getting off the ground. I knew the Ultimate Tiebreaker and Ultimate Resource strategies were sound, so where was the problem? I realized the problem lay with the networking events themselves.

THE ULTIMATE CONNECTOR

I needed to expand my network in a meaningful way if I was going to grow the quality and quantity of my business. I recently attended an event where Seth Godin, author and entrepreneur, stated, "The value of your connections is worth more than the value of your services or widgets." This is true now more than ever, and focusing on the Ultimate Tiebreaker and Ultimate Resource is a great way to make this a reality. Unfortunately, I found that large, traditional networking events afforded little opportunity to develop my capabilities as an Ultimate Tiebreaker or Ultimate Resource. I couldn't connect my clients to the best of everything they might need, because I wasn't meeting the best. I couldn't connect them to opportunities either, because the people I was meeting weren't looking for solutions the way I was. So I did the next best thing: I created my own networking group and made myself the Ultimate Connector.

I brought together a group (20-30 people) that included my clients, their key relationships and other remarkable professionals with whom I wanted to collaborate. I'm going to show you how you can develop a powerful core of connectors like this for your network as well. Using these methodologies, you can exponentially increase the success of your networking endeavors because your focus will always be on adding value for your existing clients and strategic partners.

I call this concept of forming your own networking group "CONECTOR" (what's a how-to book without a digestible mnemonic?). The next six chapters will help you under-stand the importance of creating a solid network around the best people you know, and tell you how to do more for your best clients while positioning yourself to attract more who are just like them. Here is how it breaks down:

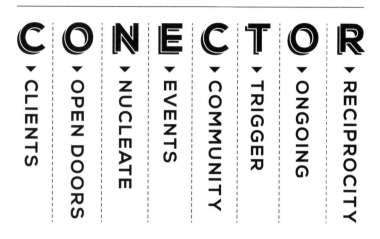

CLIENTS · OPEN DOORS · NUCLEATE · EVENTS · COMMUNITY · TRIGGER ONGOING RECIPROCITY

The professional who effectively uses both the Ultimate Tiebreaker (referring opportunities to your clients) and Ultimate Resource (providing qualified resources) strategies can easily become the Ultimate Connector (adding extraordinary value by making connections).

Building your own group is easier than you think, and my hope is that you'll follow the process I'm about to describe to do it. But even if you decide not to take this more formalized approach, there are plenty of useful tactics in the next chapters that you can apply to your business to spur growth and improve both the quality and quantity of your clients.

CHAPTER 03

CLIENTS

CLIENTS

Now that we've explored why traditional networking is not working, and how creating more value for your existing clients can be infinitely more effective in bringing more people like them to you, it's time to get down to business.

The first step is to identify who the members of your group should be. Do this by identifying your best relationships, the ones most worthy of the effort, and then learn everything you can about them. Learn more about their businesses and their personal lives. This is about getting beyond superficiality and finding out what makes the best people in your orbit tick. Yes, it takes time, but the good news is that you only need a few high-quality candidates to set everything in motion.

I began the identification process with my existing clients. I focused initially on those whose businesses I believed could most easily get value from participating; clients that I would advocate for as an Ultimate Resource and refer opportunities to as an Ultimate Tiebreaker. This initial examination yielded 5 to 10 potential group members. It was a great starting point.

The bottom line is that you only want to invest your time in the clients you love, who love you in return. Sure, you should factor in revenue, but more importantly you should consider those who value your advice and those who share your passions—be they wine, sports, opera or Star Trek. These are the clients so perfect for you, you could see yourself happily doing business with them for years.

Before reaching out to communicate the enhanced role you will now be playing for them, you'll want to get comfortable with how the conversation should flow.

IDENTIFY TRIGGERING EVENTS

While I obviously knew what my clients did for a living, I did not necessarily know how to identify resources, opportunities or connections for all of them. What's written on a business card or incorporation documents does not tell a business's full story. So, the purpose of these initial conversations was to learn more about my clients' businesses and figure out the various ways I could add value for them.

I think most of us take for granted how well our clients and advocates understand our business. I know I did. My title and the business sector I am in are fairly self-explanatory. I'm a financial advisor. I work in financial services. Because I took this view, it was no surprise, in retrospect, that most of the referrals I received early on in my business came only from clients who were asked if they could recommend a good financial advisor.

The reality is that most people do not specifically know who can solve the challenges they have, or provide what they need. John Jantsch said it best in *The Referral Engine*: "Referrals happen most naturally when two people are talking and one of the parties expresses their current pain in the neck." He goes on to suggest, "the best way to make it easy for people to refer business your way is to develop a list of 'trigger' phrases that experience tells you are the exact words your prospects utter when they need what you've got."

Rather than taking a passive approach and waiting for network referrals to come my way, I realized I could be more proactive by making clients and friends aware of the different life and business circumstances where my services might be needed. The most effective way to tease this information out was to share my trigger phrases with them. I expanded this to also include "triggering events," which are events that are not directly related to what I provide, but where I am usually able to provide a solution.

An example of a trigger phrase for me is "I have been managing my own money and don't have time to keep up with it." Whereas an example of a triggering event would be someone having a baby. They may already have a great relationship with a financial advisor, but I also know that many people become more motivated about and concerned with their financial plan once they have a child.

Here's an example: My personal trainer didn't know a lot about my professional life. He was more concerned with making sure I got in the right amount of cardio while not skimping on my strength training. However, his worldview was similar to mine. He was always looking to be helpful. He wanted to know how he could identify someone who might be in need of a good financial advisor—basically, how he could be a better connector for me, add more value, and deliver the Ultimate Tiebreaker.

Obviously, most of us would not think to ask our personal trainer—or most anyone for that matter—if he or she knows a good financial advisor. However, personal trainers have intimate conversations with their clients every day, and many of them share a lot about what is going on in their personal and professional lives. I could have just asked him to let me know if anyone mentioned they were looking for a good financial advisor. But that's very reductive, very transactional. So that's not what I did, and it's not what you should do either.

In order for him to make quality introductions to me, I didn't need for him to know all the ins and outs of my business. I needed him to know what my prospective clients were struggling with. I needed him to know who would make a good client for my firm. I needed him to be able to spot the clues that this person sweating out crunches in front of him would be a perfect introduction for Derek Coburn.

I listed out my triggering events and started sharing them with my clients and strategic partners. I let my trainer know that if someone was thinking about selling their business they were a good prospective client. If they said things like, "I really want to spend more time with my kids," that was a pretty reliable indicator. My list of triggering events also includes things like buying a home, selling a business or concerns about the health or finances of aging parents.

Once he was aware of my triggers, he was able to identify opportunities to refer great prospective clients. And he did—two of them, in fact. Do you think I would ever hire another trainer after that? Of course not, especially since I've been in my trainer's shoes in this type of situation. If you recall, this is precisely the kind of value that David the Landscaper appreciated when he chose to stick with me after meeting with the other advisor at the behest of one of his big clients.

This is who you want to be for your clients. To get there, you need to find out what their trigger phrases and triggering events are. You also need to identify your own. Ian Altman of Grow My Revenue said it best: "Don't tell people what you do, tell them what problems you solve." If you're having trouble with that, I've laid out some questions in the next section that are intended for your clients but double as a worthwhile personal exercise.

The important thing is to understand that you will significantly increase your pool of interested parties by sharing your triggering events with clients and your network. In doing so, you will also be in a much better position to help your clients do the same.

IDENTIFYING YOUR CLIENTS' TRIGGERS

The next step is reaching out to set up interviews with your clients to share your plan. I told my clients that I wanted to contribute as an extra member of their business development team. Of course they loved the idea—it was a can't-lose proposition for them.

A typical response was, "Let me get this straight: I'm not going to see any reduction in the quality of service you're providing, and on top of that you're going to learn more about my business so you can help find me more clients?" Every one of my clients was eager to have this discussion.

To kick off the interview, I shared my vision regarding the Ultimate Tiebreaker and Resource (they did not have proper names at that point). I then asked how I could better recognize a client or opportunity for them. Often this part took some time because I wasn't familiar with their industry. I needed it explained to me in terms I could easily understand and act on. It turned out, understanding their industry was as hard for me as explaining it was for them.

When I had this conversation with my clients, most of them had not thought much about how someone else could identify opportunities for them. Often they could not articulate what distinguished their business from their competitors—or what their ideal client looked like—to someone outside their industry.

EXERCISE: UNCOVERING TRIGGERING EVENTS

Going through this exercise with your clients will make you look like a hero, even if nothing else comes out of the meeting, because you've unlocked deeper understanding and better communication. This can be a bit of a double-edged sword, however. Most of your clients will assume, since you already know what they do, that you will also know how to uncover opportunities for them. But as we've discussed, this is not necessarily the case. They need to understand that while you know they are a consultant or a government contractor, you aren't necessarily sure what that means in terms of identifying potential clients for them. Here are some questions you can ask to get greater clarification:

Q. WHAT IS THE ROLE OF THE PERSON WHO TYPICALLY HIRES YOU?

Q. WHERE AND WITH WHOM DO THEY TYPICALLY SPEND THEIR TIME?

Q. WHAT PROBLEM(S) ARE THEY PRIMARILY LOOKING TO SOLVE THAT YOU CAN HELP WITH?

Q. WHAT IS THE SIZE (EMPLOYEES AND REVENUE) OF YOUR IDEAL CLIENT?

Q. WHAT ARE SOME OF THEIR TRIGGER PHRASES AND TRIGGERING EVENTS?

There are many others, but this should get you started. Not only will this information put you in a better position to identify clients for your clients, but they'll learn a lot about their messaging. They'll realize they could be much more effective at communicating not just their value proposition, but who they are and what they're looking for. And they will love you for it!

Having these conversations with my clients made them feel even better about having me in their corner. It also felt great personally. Focusing on how I could help some of my best clients was, and remains, an incredibly rewarding experience.

After taking your clients through this process, invariably they will want to know more about your triggering events. This is yet another reason it's so important to clarify your own triggering events prior to these conversations. Even if you are providing a compelling service that separates you from the pack—the essence of the Ultimate Tiebreaker—a conversation with a prospective client can only take place when they are at least somewhat interested in what you provide. Triggering events are a subject that unifies you, gives you something in common, and piques mutual interest better than almost anything.

I never mention my un-networking group during these conversations, for one reason. They are the vetting process by which I determine which clients might be a good fit. And you should do the same. It might feel weird at first—picking those who belong versus those who don't—but that is the entire point of this new networking paradigm we're developing: to add more value by finding the best fit. Besides, those who don't feel like the best fit will still benefit from *and contribute* to what you are building just by virtue of being in your larger network.

ACCESS IS AN ASSET[2]

The value of cultivating a high-quality network cannot be overemphasized. When you enlist yourself as a business development advocate for your clients, your success will depend on your ability to promote them to, and through, your network. Your network should also inspire confidence in you as a go-to resource when your clients are faced with important decisions. As you go through the exercises in this book, your network will most certainly grow in size, but your goal is for it to grow in quality as well. The higher the quality of your network, the greater the magnitude of your success.

The key is to make sure your clients know about it. I let my clients know that as my network was growing, I was meeting more and more professionals who could be potential clients or business allies. I made sure to point out that they were successful *and* well-connected, which helped instill even more confidence in me because the assets I brought to our relationship didn't end at the

---

2   "Access Is an Asset" is a term coined by master connector Chris Brogan. As he put it in a blog post, "Building access is every bit as important as learning or earning." Chris always has great advice on connecting and building relationships. These days he mostly writes for Owner Magazine (which he founded). I highly encourage you to sign up for it at www.ownermag.com.

services I provided, but extended to access to a growing, high-quality network of business professionals.

For extra rock star points, I told each of my clients that I wanted them to spend more time growing their business, hanging out with their family, or doing whatever else was important to them. And I meant it. If I could make their day-to-day decisions easier—by taking the stress of finding a new mechanic or nanny off their plate, for instance—I was adding more value to our relationship. This is part of what it means to be an Ultimate Resource.

To earn both my Ultimate Tiebreaker and Ultimate Resource badges with clients, I needed to know more not only about their ideal clients, but also what was going on in their businesses and in their lives. Were they looking to acquire another company? Develop a more effective web presence? Find a good sushi restaurant? If I could help them solve any of these problems by farming my network for the best available options, I could potentially be a more effective resource for one client while creating opportunities for another. It's a win-win scenario.

If you follow this process, your clients will be more than excited and appreciative of your efforts. In all likelihood they will also support what you're building, even if it takes a little time.

GROWING YOUR BASE

↑↑↑

Once I gathered the information I needed about my clients' ideal clients, I asked them for connections to a few of the other businesses with whom they interacted. Specifically, I was looking for a simple introduction to the ones they held in the highest regard, the cream of the crop.

This wasn't rocket science. It was as simple as asking if they knew of two or three professionals who were just plain awesome. Was their accountant brilliant? Did their daughter's piano teacher have her playing Chopin in no time? Were they wowed by the movers they hired to get them into their new place? Or the realtor who sold it to them?

Your clients should be receptive to your ask at this point, because you will have already established the immense value you bring to your business relationships. Even if your clients don't fully understand that connecting you with a few of their key professional contacts will help make you an even better resource for *them,* they will almost certainly recognize that they are doing a favor for both sides of the introduction; which is, itself, a valuable act. And of course, getting introduced to these individuals is a great starting point for expanding your network and increasing the pool of candidates from which to form your un-networking group.

Please note, however, that it is unlikely you'll be able to build your group exclusively around existing clients. Even if you think you can, I would encourage you to hold off on trying. It is not an ideal approach. For now, let's take a look at how to expand the pool of your network—and the prospective members for your un-networking group—in a way that will increase your ability to add value for your clients and develop relationships with some of the top professionals in your area.

CHAPTER 04

OPENING DOORS

OPENING DOORS

The single most important thing you can do at this stage is expand your network to include the best professionals in your area. When I started, I wasn't in a position to provide regular introductions for my clients or solutions for every request they made. My network just wasn't big enough. To truly deliver on the promises I made to my clients, I needed to get on the radar of the very best professionals in my area and develop relationships.

In addition to quality, variety is important. If your goal is to add as much value as possible, it does you little good to go an inch wide and a mile deep. Knowing *all* the lawyers in town, for instance, doesn't make you a resource; it makes you a subject matter expert. So be sure to connect with the best in a variety of professions. This way you can make great recommendations no matter the circumstance. The last thing you want is to come up empty-handed when a client turns to you as a resource. It can cost you credibility and they may hesitate to reach out the next time they need something.

In an ideal world you would have strategic relationships with other professionals who can make you look like a hero and reciprocate your efforts. If you implement all of the strategies in this book, odds are you will. But it isn't time for that yet. Right now it's all about adding value for your clients by leveraging the expertise and talents of the very best people and businesses in town. The first step is to identify and connect with them.

EXPANDING THE QUANTITY AND QUALITY OF YOUR NETWORK

There are three primary outlets to expand your professional network: recommendations from your clients, reconnecting with those in your own network with whom you already have relationships, and identifying and connecting with those you have yet to meet.

Your interactions and conversations *will* vary slightly between each unique segment, and I will review how each conversation should differ. However, your primary objective in every case will be the same: to identify and engage with these individuals and determine (in this order):

1) If they have a great business that could add more value for your existing (and future) clients, should they ever have a need

2) If they share your worldview on developing relationships with other professionals (the first litmus test for their addition to your networking group)

3) What issues or problems they currently have that you could help them solve (ideally by introducing them to one of your clients)

You will talk with professionals who are not a great fit for your network based on the above criteria. That's okay. There is no light without dark, no hot without cold. If everyone were equally valuable in a business context, we wouldn't be spending so much time lamenting the fallow ground of large networking events. Of course, these less ideal professional contacts could still deliver a great experience for one of your clients down the road the next time they ask you for a recommendation, so don't be too quick to chuck that valuable arrow from your quiver.

My doctor is a good example. He has a waiting list for new patients and therefore no pressing need to expand his network. However, if a client of mine needs a great doctor and I can get him bumped to the top of the list, I have created value for both parties. For my client because I filled an immediate need with a high-quality expert. For my doctor because I connected him to a lower risk, pre-vetted client (by virtue of our relationship).

Eventually, you'll only want to focus your time and efforts on professionals who align perfectly with you and your business. It is much easier to collaborate and add value for each other when you play in the same space.

There are also a few key things to look for when determining whether someone is a good fit.

IDEAL NETWORKING PROFILE

So many resources offer invaluable advice around the idea of establishing your ideal client profile (i.e. *Getting Clients, Keeping Clients*, which is industry-specific to financial advisors, and *The Pumpkin Plan* by Mike Michalowicz, to name a few). As I shared earlier, I am a big fan of going through this process of establishing minimums and attracting clients with shared interests.

However, not much has been provided in terms of focusing your networking efforts around other professionals who are aligned with you. When first starting out, we are likely to take on just about anyone as a client. As we grow and have more options, we tend to be more selective.

The process of identifying who deserves to be in your network should be no different. In the beginning, you'd have anyone who would have you. As your business and network grow, your focus should be on establishing relationships only with high-quality professionals. High quality doesn't always translate into ideal, however.

FIND OTHER GO-GIVERS [3]

The first step is identifying people with high-quality businesses. Once you've connected with a person who has a world-class business you would feel comfortable referring to your clients, you need to take the additional step of determining whether they're ideal for *your* purposes. Gauge whether they're predisposed to collaborating with other professionals strictly for their own benefit, or to improve their relationships with their clients. Are they wired as a helpful, pay-it-forward person, or do they merely *think* they are? Based on my own experiences, this can be the hardest thing to figure out.

If you ask someone point blank if they are referable or if they seek to help their clients solve problems outside their area of expertise, of course they will say yes. Why wouldn't they? Whether it's dishonesty or self-delusion, no one is going to respond with a big fat honest "No."

One important tip to help distinguish the haves from the

---

3 "Go-Giver" is a term coined by Bob Burg and John David Mann in their classic book *The Go-Giver: A Little Story about a Powerful Business Idea*. It means adding value to others in a way that helps them significantly while at the same time both increasing your own sense of joy and improving your bottom line.

have-nots: Don't lead them with your questioning. Let them tell you how they conduct their business and how they deal with others. Ask for specifics. Here are some of the questions I ask to get clarity around how they are wired:

Q. HOW OFTEN DO YOUR CLIENTS ASK YOU FOR RECOMMENDATIONS?

Q. WHAT TYPES OF RECOMMENDATIONS (INDUS-TRIES, NEEDS, ETC.) DO THEY TURN TO YOU FOR? ASK FOR AN EXAMPLE OR TWO.

Q. WHAT ARE YOUR EXPECTATIONS WHEN YOU REFER A CLIENT TO ANOTHER PROFESSIONAL?

Q. WHAT HAS WORKED OR NOT WORKED WITH OTHER PROFESSIONALS IN THE PAST IN TERMS OF GIVING AND GETTING REFERRALS?

Q. HAVE YOU EVER REFERRED A CLIENT TO A FI-NANCIAL ADVISOR (USE YOUR INDUSTRY) AND HOW DID THAT OPPORTUNITY COME ABOUT?

Q. WHAT DO YOU LIKE OR DISLIKE ABOUT OTHER FINANCIAL ADVISORS (USE YOUR INDUSTRY)?

The information you gather from this line of questioning will be incredibly valuable when vetting potential members of your group.

Now that you have a good idea what to cover when you eventually converse with these folks, let's look at the differences in how you will connect and interact with those in each unique category.

CLIENT RECOMMENDATIONS

Once you have communicated to your existing clients your plan to take your relationship to new heights and compiled a list of remarkable professionals, it's time to build out your un-networking group to include people you don't know.

The ideal scenario is to have your clients introduce you via email. If they agree, make it easy for them! Create an email template that all of your clients can use, which frames the introduction in a way that benefits both you and your client. Making it simple for them shows that you appreciate the value of their time—and of course, increases the likelihood that they'll follow through...

If for whatever reason you need to send the email yourself, just explain to them that your client suggested they meet with you in order to pursue a collaboration that could potentially benefit you both.

In talking to professionals with whom you share clients, remember that your top priority (even more important than gathering the information outlined above) should be exploring how you can add value for these mutual clients. Even if the person you're talking to does not turn out to be a fit for the group you're forming, these discussions will likely unearth ways to improve your shared client relationships.

Create a spreadsheet of the individuals you connect with through your clients' recommendations. Include columns for each person's name, industry and notes. Then highlight the ones you think could be right for your group, or worth developing a relationship with. You should have a good list at this point, but we still have some work to do.

A free sample template with examples of what the spreadsheet should look like is available at:

WWW.DEREKCOBURN.COM/BOOKTEMPLATES

YOUR EXISTING NETWORK

To clarify, your existing network is comprised of the individuals you have met and kept in touch with over the years. Some you will know well, others may have fallen through the cracks. Either way, you should only reach out to those you believe can contribute to your network.

There is no need to pre-screen anyone you already feel really good about. Go ahead and add them to your spreadsheet. Only contact the ones you're unsure about. At the very least, this will give you an opportunity to catch up and fill them in on the new approach you're taking with your business. Some will be intrigued and ask a lot of questions—a great way to gauge whether your approach is resonating (and if this person belongs on your list after all).

FILLING IN THE GAPS

You should have an impressive list compiled at this point, but there's no need to worry if you don't. Either way, you will want to target additional people. While putting together your group, or building your network in general, it's important to have a good sense for which industries you want represented. These will differ depending on your profession.

As a financial advisor, I knew I wanted to have relationships with professionals who talked with clients about their money: accountants, attorneys, bankers, etc. They would be at the center of my network (and my networking group).

What are the primary industries or professions that should be represented in your group? For example, if you're a B2B business and deal primarily with CFOs, you'll want to develop relationships with others who work directly with CFOs. Think about what other industries or types of professionals have been good sources of introductions for you in the past. Which industries are going to be useful to your clients? Take a moment and write down what comes to mind.

Now check this list against the list of connections you've compiled and vetted. Are there any omissions or redundancies? For example, if you have three IT professionals on your list, don't worry about meeting any more. On the other hand if you don't have a single attorney, you might need to find one.

You'll want to round out your network with people in professions that are not related directly to yours. Of course you should target certain relevant industries, but these days being well-connected and influential are more important factors than relevance or sector alignment because great introductions tend to come from people who are well regarded in your community. I have received some of my best client introductions from an interior designer, an eye surgeon, and, of course, my personal trainer.

If you still need to add more quality people to your growing network—never a bad idea—you'll need to do some legwork. Thankfully, the web and social media in particular make this a lot easier than it has ever been.

LINKEDIN: You can use LinkedIn to find top professionals in your area in almost any industry. Start with people you are connected to and then look for introductions to their connections. One of the great things about LinkedIn is that you can search by industries, connections or regions. Think about all the industries in which you have been asked for recommendations. Review your spreadsheet to see if any industries you know will be valuable to your network are absent. Then target those on LinkedIn. Start by searching industries and filter the results based on your 2nd degree connections. If you share at least one connection, you lower the risk of coming off as a spammer. After you find the right people, or at least someone you think would be a fit for your group, make contact.

You can ask one of your common connections for an introduction, or reach out directly. Let them know who you are and that your clients have looked, or may be looking, for someone who does what they do. I like to let them know that in the last year or two, I've had clients ask me for a referral to someone within that person's industry and I had no one to refer them to (assuming this is true). I also let them know that I aim to be a resource for my clients and I'd like to know more about what they do and who they serve best, so the next time a client asks me for a referral, I'll know if they're a good fit. Then see if they would be receptive to setting up a quick call to discuss. Based on my experience, if you use this approach, you should be able to set up calls with 90% of the folks you contact.

On that first call, be sure to share your approach to business and connecting people, and explain how this benefits your clients. Avoid bringing up your business. If you lead with your business, they will think your reaching out was just a gimmick. That's obviously not the impression you want to give. If the person on the other end is the type of person you're looking for, they will most likely ask about your business anyway. In fact, this is a good way to tell if you are talking to someone worth developing a relationship with.[4]

TWITTER: Twitter can be an excellent tool for finding people. A lot of my colleagues go on the defensive at the mention of social networking, saying they don't have time to be on LinkedIn or Facebook or Twitter. Whether I believe them or not is beside the point (FYI, I don't). What matters is that I can spend 10 minutes a night on these platforms and share ideas with minimal effort that connect me to potential contacts. Compare that to spending hours at a big networking event, which requires much more effort and is, quite frankly, a total crapshoot.

Online, you have total control of who talks to you, who you start conversations with, and who you continue conversations with. You can see who and what people are talking about. You can directly follow the leaders and professionals you want to meet. You can see what they are up to

---

4   If you want to learn more about using LinkedIn to grow your network, I highly recommend *Linked Working* by Lewis Howes.

and discern from who they know and what they talk about whether they might contribute to your network. If you can, chime in. Retweet them. Comment positively to your followers *about* them, using their Twitter handle. Many times this is enough to grab their attention and get on their radar.

Again, don't lead with your business. You already know this is not a good approach for networking events–yet this is where many people go wrong on Twitter. I follow a simple rule of thumb for social media: I never do online what I would not do in real life.[5]

THE NEXT LEVEL

Now that you have a vetted list of the people you've met, whether previously or more recently through introductions from your clients, it's time to figure out who's going to board your un-networking train. You don't have time to deepen your relationships with all of these individuals, so the next step is to thin the ranks and identify the most worthy.

---

5   My favorite book about meeting people and growing your network on Twitter is *The Tao of Twitter* by Mark Schaefer. Whether you will be trying out Twitter for the first time, or have been using it for years, this book is an invaluable resource.

CHAPTER 05

NUCLEATE

NUCLEATE

A successful networking group, or networking strategy, requires you to be at the center. You need to be the nucleus. In Webster's words, you need to be the "central and most important part of an object, movement, or group...forming the basis for its activity and growth." Do not mistake this for meaning it's all about you; rather, it's about you connecting all of the links, like the hub of a wheel.

ANOTHER NETWORKING GROUP? YOU MUST BE JOKING

At this point you're well on your way to building a powerful network that will serve your clients well and, ultimately, grow your business. But before you storm the castle, there's an important question to consider: Why would anyone be interested? Even if you've done a good job compiling a roster of highly successful and ideal professionals, they will probably have the same negative feelings about networking groups and events as you do. In fact, it's not only probable. You can be sure of it, because you wouldn't be interested in them if they didn't. Like you, they are busy, their time is extremely valuable, and they've soured on the traditional approach to networking–so you can anticipate an objection. To take a page out of Sales 101, you'll need to meet this objection and communicate the value you will be creating. Because why on God's green earth would they want to get involved with another networking group?

The answer, of course, is that this is not just another networking group. For starters, you will have carefully vetted everyone involved based on a three-part rubric: 1) the quality of their business, 2) their ability to help or connect, and 3) their willingness to do so. While I am not a fan of the "pay it forward" approach with individuals I don't know well, I do know that if you create an environment made up exclusively of people wired like this, great things happen organically.[6]

---

6 I know this from personal experience with my 100-person CEO-level networking group called "cadre." I see it happen for those dedicated professionals every day.

PAINT A NEW PICTURE

↻

You need to paint a different picture for them. Communicate that the people you're bringing together genuinely like making connections and have a "How can I help?" approach to developing relationships. This group will be playing by a different set of rules (Number One: no direct solicitation allowed). The focus will be on interacting with people who do not view the group as a source of leads, but rather as a platform for meeting other successful professionals who are interested in how they can help each other.

When you're ready to invite your A-list people to take part in your group, you want to be clear about what exactly you're inviting them into and get their buy-in. This one is not optional. You've heard the expression, "one bad apple spoils the whole bunch"? It grew out of situations like this, where one naysayer ruins the energy created by an entire group. We've talked about vetting people, but this is a good juncture for looking more deeply at who fits the profile of an "un-networker."

INTENTIONS REVISITED

↻

The success that comes out of any professional group cor-
relates directly with how similar the quality and intentions
are of the professionals within that group. In order for your
network to be effective, you must be selective about who you
surround yourself with. How do they approach networking?
Are they influential? What is their intention when making an
introduction? Do their ideal clients look like your ideal clients?
Are they willing to make time to engage and contribute?

We talked about intentions in Chapter 1. One of the main
reasons networking is not working is that so many people
approach it with a "What can you do for me?" mindset.
If your primary focus is on adding value for your existing
clients and others in your network, but you're interacting
with folks who are primarily looking for business, there will
be a disconnect. You have to be sincere about wanting to
help the people you know and trust—and every member
of your group will have to be equally sincere about helping
the people you're about to connect them with.

Consider the pitfalls we discussed earlier too. They are
very real, as I'm sure we can all attest to, and now you

have a responsibility to make sure no one you bring into your group runs into any of them. We know how it plays out when the person on the other end of a connection does not share your mindset. A lack of generosity, or even common courtesy, can leave a seriously bad taste in your mouth.

In the past when I was referring clients to other professionals, I ran into my fair share of challenges. Some went well, but most did not. Sometimes the person I referred didn't keep me updated on their interactions with my clients. Sometimes I never got so much as a thank you. Other times they didn't respond to my introduction at all. (Who is so busy they can't respond to a potential opportunity?!) I don't know about you, but I'm thrilled when I get a referral from someone in my network. I respond right away to thank them. Even if the referral is less than ideal, I still express my appreciation and use this as an opportunity to clarify what would make a great referral for me. Communication is essential.

Make no mistake: When you're exploring new relationships with strategic partners, it is hard to find people who are aligned with your vision and share your mindset. At first, most of the people you invite to join will take you up on your offer, but whether they stick around depends almost entirely on the quality and engagement of everyone else involved.

This is an especially important point when it comes to your own reputation because part of what you are "selling" is comfort and curation. You have handpicked every professional in the group and, because of this, everyone can let their guard down a bit. No one is going to hear anyone's sales pitch. You are endeavoring to create a transfer of trust that allows everyone to feel more comfortable working with the members of your group, much more so than if they had met them randomly. This is what differentiates your group from the crowd. If you make exceptions or invite people who are not committed to contributing to the overall effort, you will lose trust and damage your reputation, neither of which is easy to rebuild.

IDENTIFY THE CREAM OF THE CROP

In order to create the ideal networking group, you need people who want the same things you do. People who will keep you in the loop and help you be a better resource, while also giving you the opportunity to help them. With the right people in your group, you can open more doors for everyone—including yourself.

Based on all of your prep work, by now you should have a good idea who you would like to invite. Assuming they meet all of your criteria, there is one other thing to consider: How effective are they in telling their story and communicating how others can help them? Have they identified their triggering events? Do they know what their ideal clients look like? They need to be able to make it easy for the other members of the group to help them. Someone can be world-class at what they do, but let's face it, if they can't effectively communicate what differentiates them, no one is going to be inspired to move mountains on their behalf. Just as you have learned to differentiate yourself and make it easy for others to help, you want the people you bring into your group to do the same.

I would also think twice before inviting someone who seems difficult to help. This is something that the vetting process described in Chapters 3 and 4 is designed to sniff out: If someone has trouble identifying who their ideal clients are or describing their business in a way that differentiates it, that's a red flag. However, it is not a total deal breaker. You can still add value, namely by helping them express how others can identify opportunities for them. If someone seems like a good fit but needs help with their story, walk them through the process for uncovering triggering events.

After using these last few criteria to fine-tune your list, you should select the best 20-30 individuals to invite into your circle. This means you have some decisions to make. When narrowing down your list, make someone's ability to directly add value for your existing clients the deciding factor. It's okay if you leave some good people off your initial invitation list; you can always use them as alternates.

It is also not the end of the world if you misjudge a few of the first people you invite. You have a good handle on what to look for, and you've done your best to select the right people. If the majority of them get it and are adding value, no one will hold it against you if there are a few slackers at the start. You will want to reconfirm their intentions after a fair amount of time, however, and if they don't step up, they should not be invited back.

REACHING OUT

Now that you've assembled your own cadre of remarkable professionals, you're ready to nucleate and start connecting them.

Start by sending out an email communicating that you're in the process of creating an intimate networking community comprised of professionals who are committed to developing meaningful, mutually beneficial relationships with likeminded people.

Share your vision. Make the initial recipients of your email understand that by inviting the right people and leading events, as well as facilitating the connections that come out of them (which we'll get to in a moment), you're going to make it easy for them to focus on becoming an advocate for others in the group. And, because you've taken great care to vet all of your members, they can be confident that everyone in the group is willing to be an advocate for them.

You should use a good combination of online and offline interactions to engage with your network, but in my experience the best way to kick things off is with high-quality in-person events.

CHAPTER 06

EVENTS

EVENTS

Once you've identified the core of your group and established yourself as its nucleus, it's time to make the magic happen. That means Events with a capital "E." This is where you bring to life the antithesis of the standard, time-sucking networking events everyone knows and hates.

Used effectively, events—the ones you host, and the ones you attend—can become a major factor in your success. I have found that the perfect way to bring together a great group of people is to hold a lunch event. Before you roll your eyes, let me assure you that this is not the one-on-one lunch that occasionally comes out of meeting someone at a networking event. You know that drill: You meet up, and you end up wasting your time listening to someone's sales pitch.

This is something completely different. What I am suggesting is a way to host a platform for fostering ongoing relationships and creating valuable opportunities for everyone involved. That just happens to be over food in the middle of the day.

LUNCH: THE MOST IMPORTANT MEAL OF YOUR DAY

Assuming you have around 20 people in your group, you should start by hosting two lunches a month with spots for 10 at each one. By planning two events, you give your members options and increase the likelihood that they will work one of your lunches into their busy schedules.

While eventually these lunches will become a forum for deepening relationships, the initial goal will be to get everyone acquainted. Essentially, you will facilitate a roundtable discussion in which each attendee takes 5-7 minutes to introduce themselves and their business to the others.

Of course, scheduling two (and eventually more) lunches a

month for 20 to 30 super-busy business leaders involves some logistics. But don't freak out. I've been hosting these events for years, and I've made many mistakes. I learned the hard way—now you won't have to.

SELECTING RESTAURANTS

Once you know who you're going to invite, it's time to pick one or two venues. Let locale dictate your restaurant choice (you can indulge your foodie habits on your own time). If, like me, you live in a city where things are more spread out, choose restaurants in two different parts of the city where most of the people on your list are concentrated.

Now, what makes for a good power lunch venue? In order to make this a positive and productive experience for everyone, make sure the restaurant has the following:

- **A professional clientele and wait staff.** Since your party will likely consist of CEOs and thought leaders, make sure the restaurant caters to this market.

- **A private room.** This is non-negotiable. If you're sitting at a table large enough for 10-15 people in the middle of a restaurant, it will be difficult to hear each other over the lunchtime din. Make sure you have some privacy so your attendees can focus on the conversation.

TIP: When you're looking to book a private room, find out the restaurant's food and beverage minimum (especially around the holidays). If a restaurant requires a minimum and you like everything else about it, you can usually get this waived by breaking it down like this: "I want to bring in 20 CEOs twice a month, and I'll give you a chance to pitch your business to them before we eat." Not a bad deal for a smart GM who caters to the business crowd.

- **Separate checks.** Unless you plan to cover the cost for everyone (which I don't recommend, and no one will expect), you will want to make sure the restaurant is able to accommodate separate checks for each guest. I once hosted a lunch where the servers were so disorganized it took them 30 minutes to get everyone's check right. To avoid this embarrassment, call ahead. Most restaurants will be fine with it. If they have any hesitation, make sure they feel comfortable accommodating this request before you make a reservation.

You should try out all of the restaurants you're considering. Even if you've been to them before, you'll be looking at different things with your roundtable lunch in mind. You'll want to gauge how they handle volume, for instance, so there are no surprises (hopefully). Being a regular patron will also put you in a better position to command the attention of the owner/GM/events coordinator on the day of your event. If there's anyone you want on your side as your guests start filtering in, it's them!

One thing to look out for specifically is distractions. It goes without saying that they should be minimal. Is there street construction going on outside? Do the servers talk loudly, forget to close the door to your private room, or get orders mixed up? A slip up of this sort can quickly change the mood of your lunch. On the day of the event, arrive early and communicate your expectations to the people who will be handling things.

SCHEDULING YOUR LUNCHES

Once you've determined the location, it's time to invite your group. Finding times that work for 20-30 busy professionals may seem daunting, but there are many tools out there that make scheduling easier than you'd think. One of my favorites is Doodle (www.doodle.com). This allows you to offer multiple scheduling options and get Yes/No/Maybe responses from your invitees.

List the dates, times and locations of both events, and ask everyone to confirm their availability (or lack thereof) for each. Ask them to reply by a specific day and time (this should be within 48 hours), and let them know that you will be following up with a formal invitation.

When you have all of your responses, you should be able to form two groups of approximately 10 people for each event (assuming you've invited 20 people total). You'll be assigning them to events primarily based on their availability, but if someone is available for both events, you can use other criteria such as their industry or role in order to create a good mix of professionals at each event.

PREPPING YOUR GUESTS

When you send out your formal invitations with the final date and time for each group/event, be sure to include some loose guidelines. Let your guests know they will each have 5-7 minutes (pick a time allotment based on the number of attendees) to address the group, and suggest they cover any or all of the following:

- THEIR NAME AND THEIR BUSINESS

- A DESCRIPTION OF THEIR IDEAL CLIENT/ OPPORTUNITY (NOT WHAT THEY DO)

- A RECENT SUCCESS STORY, OR PROBLEM THEY HELPED RESOLVE

- HOW THE GROUP CAN IDENTIFY POTENTIAL OPPORTUNITIES FOR THEM

- WHAT TYPES OF PROFESSIONALS SHARE THE SAME CLIENTELE

- ANY EVENTS/CAUSES THEY ARE CURRENTLY INVOLVED WITH

- OTHER ORGANIZATIONS THEY ARE INVOLVED WITH (BOARDS, CHARITIES, ETC.)

- A FEW PERSONAL DETAILS (FAMILY, HOBBIES, ETC.)

This will keep everyone on the same page and give them a common language to speak throughout the course of the lunch.

FACILITATING CONNECTIONS

In order to really make sure these lunches are as productive as possible, you need to do some homework on your attendees. Since you have already completed the vetting process, you should know the basics of what each person does, what they look for in a client, etc. But prior to the lunch you'll want to fill in any gaps, particularly on the topics you've suggested they talk to the group about. Are they passionate about a certain charity? Do they play tennis? You need to know these things so that if they leave something out, you can come in, tag-team style, to make sure their full stories get told.

TIP: To prevent people from going over their allotted time, I recommend using an app called Talk Timer. I have this on my tablet and place it within the speaker's view. The screen stays solid green until one minute remaining, when it turns yellow, then red when time is up. This lets the speaker always know where they stand, and prevents you from having to interrupt. Holding everyone to their allotted time will benefit the entire group, including the people with a tendency to go long. Go beyond 5-7 minutes and you're bound to lose the group's attention. This tool prevents that.

At these lunch events, I keep my notes on each member in front of me. I recommend doing the same. You want to make sure you can help out if someone gets off track or forgets to mention something important (just about everyone will). Yes, you are there to make connections for yourself—and you will get your turn—but you will also need to manage the flow of conversation. You should encourage everyone to ask follow-up questions and chime in if they have something to add. The best way to do that well is with good notes.

Each participant's talk should cover areas in which they could use some help. As you go around the table, be sure to note when others offer help in real time. These are potential connections, and it's going to be your job to facilitate their growth from potential to *actual.*

RINSE, REPEAT

↻

After hosting your first couple of lunches, start keeping track of which members have met. In the earlier days of your un-networking group, you want your members to rotate around so they are always meeting new people. Ultimately everyone should meet at least once before you start tinkering with the guest list. Tracking connections will help you assign members to the next phase of lunches, where your objective will be to arrange things so that members who have connected at previous lunches get the opportunity to reconnect and deepen their relationships.

After a few months, as those relationships have started to develop in earnest, you can encourage your regular attend-ees to invite other people from outside of the group. These guests may not be a great fit *per se*, but giving your members the opportunity to invite their best clients and connections to an exclusive lunch with 10 remarkable professionals is a great way to add value both for them and your group.

ATTENDING OTHER EVENTS: THE RIGHT TIME AND THE RIGHT PLACE

As I'm sure I've conveyed to you by now, I am not a fan of randomly attending larger networking events. However, there are some occasions when you can leverage these events to strategically benefit your network.

If there's an upcoming function you're obligated to attend, or that's featuring a great speaker, consider inviting a strategically selected subset of clients and members from your un-networking group. Remember, this strategy is all about adding value for your existing clients and professional relationships, and sometimes these larger events offer the best forum for delivering it.

LUCK = OPPORTUNITY + PREPARATION

We all have clients and friends in our network we want to introduce to each other but have never found the right opportunity to connect. Most of the time there is no pressing issue that warrants an introduction, so we sit back, wary of being that person who insists on jamming a square peg into a round hole. Still, we recognize the value of bringing these people together, so how do we make it happen? An event can present a golden opportunity to facilitate the connection.

Let's say the CPA in my group, Debbie, is a rock star who specializes in working with attorneys. My client, Charlie, is an attorney who would be better off working with Debbie than his existing accountant because of her expertise in the types of retirement plans offered by his firm.

There is one small problem: Charlie is more or less happy with his CPA. Maybe he even agrees he would be better off working with Debbie, but his existing CPA is fine and he, like most of us, doesn't feel like switching firms. In a situation like this, you don't want to force the issue because overall Charlie's doing all right. Besides, if you're constantly sending these types of requests through your network, it's the quickest way to go from being a resource to being an annoyance.

However, if I am going to a charity event that Charlie is also attending, I could invite Debbie and make an introduction there. This way, I am creating an opportunity for her to make a good impression and earn permission to follow up with Charlie in the future.

Remember, when you do something like this you have to be authentic and approach the situation with the sincere intention of helping *both* parties. I would not facilitate this introduction just to help Debbie—and certainly not because I was looking for Debbie to return the favor. I have to truly believe that Charlie would be better off working with Debbie (if things even got that far). Since his current advisor is good enough, it would not make sense to push the connection. The best thing to do is put the ball in Debbie's court, since she is someone I can trust to approach developing a relationship the right way.

Obviously your hopes in these scenarios are for your friends and clients to click, develop relationships, and grow more successful. Understand, however, that you cannot make this happen. You can only create an opportunity for them and expect that they are prepared both to recognize and seize it. That is the essence of the un-networking model.

THE BUSY AND POWERFUL

Larger events can also be the best places for you to introduce people in your group to some of your more prestigious connections. If you're like me, you have a few powerful, influential people in your network. They're smart, they're leaders in their industry and community, and like most powerful and influential people, they have targets on their backs. Everyone wants a piece of them at events and they are usually approached by people who are only looking to get their business.

Fortunately for you and your un-networking connections, it is different when you engage with this type of person. They already know and trust you, and they will be receptive when you offer to make a valuable connection for them. You're selective and this isn't something you approach them with every day.

Typically when people ask you for an introduction, they won't give you much to work with. They are likely vendors who want to replace the incumbent and get a shot at this person's highly sought-after business. These individuals may be your clients or members of your un-networking group, and they may well be a better option. You would like to help them, but you can't just email your ultra-valuable connections every time someone wants an introduction. You have to respect them and their time. It's the only way to preserve your relationship.

When I get these requests and I think the introduction could benefit both parties, I tell my client/group member to wait for the next larger event that I know this person will be attending. When the event rolls around, I let them know and encourage them to attend so I can make a face-to-face introduction.

With a powerful, prestigious connection you almost always want to make introductions face to face. Email strips tone and emotion out of your message. Many influential people delegate their email correspondence altogether, which means your message is more likely to fall on deaf ears. Face-to-face introductions at large networking events, alternately, offer several advantages: 1) you can convey your feelings about the other person much more directly and convincingly, 2) you can expect they will be more receptive since that's kind of why you're all at one of these events in the first place, and 3) as a trusted connection, you are a safe port in the storm of a typical networking event.

THE HOST WITH THE MOST

If, like me, you are underwhelmed by the current networking event landscape, consider hosting your own larger events. By having control over who attends, you will not have to worry about whether you're meeting the right people, nor will you have to wait for other people's schedules to align so you can introduce them, like with industry events. Here's an example that highlights the power of hosting your own gatherings:

My friend Tien Wong is a legendary entrepreneur and investor in the Washington, D.C., area. Currently, he is the CEO of Tech2000, a mobile content management software company. I won't go into his resume—the list of accomplishments is impressive—what is important is that Tien adds a lot of value for his clients by hosting great events.

Tien is passionate about bringing together clients, partners, potential clients, potential partners and all sorts of people from the community. He puts together events ranging from a Guys Night Out with cigars, steaks and scotch, to an all-out entrepreneur program featuring major venture capitalists talking about the latest trends from Main Street to Wall Street.

Anyone looking for a software company can Google what they need and find dozens of companies that provide the same service as Tech2000. But all those things being equal, if you can work with a company led by a guy like Tien, who honestly enjoys connecting you and your company with thought leaders, potential clients and good scotch, why would you consider working with any other company?

Obviously, these events would not work if Tien wasn't in a position to be helpful. And they certainly wouldn't work if Tech2000 was not a best-of-breed software company. But for Tien, these events usually break the tie with his primary competitors because of the additional value he brings to the table as a connector.

Sometimes, though, hosting an entire event is not in the cards. Maybe you're just starting out or your budget doesn't allow for the expense. There is no shame in this, and don't worry, because there is another approach: you can host a group at a hosted event.

We all attend events to support some of our favorite clients and charities: auctions, dinners, awards, conferences, etc. One way to make these events more worthwhile is to attend them with a group. (I'll share some other ways you can leverage events in Chapter 8.) Whether it's buying a table at a gala, or sponsoring a foursome of golf, think about how you can utilize your invitations to create potentially meaningful connections. I have done this on a number of occasions to bring the Charlies and Debbies of my network together. Worst-case scenario is Charlie is appreciative of your effort. Best-case scenario is they end up working together (and both of them love you for it)!

Now you have some new ideas to consider regarding events—the ones you host yourself and the ones you attend. Here's the next thing to consider: If you do not have a well thought-out process for staying in touch with the people you meet and connect at events, you are still wasting your time.

CHAPTER 07

COMMUNITY

COMMUNITY

People lose valuable relationships and opportunities all the time because their current networking strategy (if they even have one) lacks a sense of community.

When it comes to developing meaningful, lasting professional relationships, one of the biggest hurdles is staying on the top of people's minds. When you make a connection, even with someone who is genuinely willing to help you, it's rare that they have an opportunity for you right at that moment. When something comes up six months later, will they remember you? Will they know where to find you?

Most people don't have a good system for keeping track of people they meet. Even if you do, the chances are pretty good that the other person doesn't, and it takes two to tango.

So how do you fix that?

FOLLOWING UP

One of the biggest wastes of time and opportunity in networking occurs when people make quality connections and don't follow up. It is even worse to let this happen within your own group after you've raised expectations. You have to make sure it doesn't.

I learned this with one of the first lunches I hosted. The energy in the room was electric and potential connections and opportunities were flying across the table. Five days later I followed up with everyone, only to learn that hardly any of them had done follow-up of their own. This was frustrating for me, so I decided to provide a friendly kick in the butt.

Because I had taken detailed notes during the lunch, I had a good idea of who was able to help whom. I sent 30+ emails reconnecting two people at a time. They went something like this: "Rick—Just checking in to see if you followed up with Jill regarding her offer to introduce you to the CEO of xxx company you wanted to engage with."

The results were incredibly eye opening: Over 15 follow-up meetings were scheduled. Three new prospective client introductions were made, and three individuals hired someone in the group!

This step, which helps to foster a community among your group members, turned out to be crucial. It proved to me that even the most motivated and well-intentioned people might need a nudge when it comes to following up. Once they saw how willing everyone was to help, they started to realize the group's value even more—and I didn't have to be so involved after future lunches.

Even better, because *they* were the ones who dropped the post-lunch ball, they understood that I was the connector who made all of this possible. The lunches and the group worked because I was legitimately focused on adding value for my community and making sure their connections were beneficial. And they loved me for it!

If you keep track of the conversations and interactions taking place at your lunches—and by now you'll know what to look for—you can enhance your value to the group with minimal additional effort. Facilitating the deepening of connections and making sure they're seen all the way through can be as simple as sending out reminder emails. Properly worded with clear action steps, these help solidify relationships and bring about opportunities that might otherwise have fallen through the cracks. And, there are some excellent timesaving tools out there to help if, like most of us, this part of the process doesn't come naturally to you.

TOOLS OF ENGAGEMENT

Even if you're good at staying in touch with all of your important clients and contacts, it's unlikely your fellow networkers are as organized. That's just human nature; even the best of us have lapses. After you've spent time with someone at an event or meeting, will they remember you when an opportunity arises in the future? If so, will they know where to find your contact info? Will they go to the trouble of looking for it? If not, why go to networking events or schedule follow-up meetings at all?

When I first formed my group, I had to spend a lot of time setting up my own systems and rules for following up. Fortunately, a number of services have come out since then that make it a lot easier. You can use any of these to stay in touch with your network regardless of whether you've put together a formal group.

SANEBOX: I send a lot of emails that require a response, and like most of us, I do not always get one. I recently discovered a tool called SaneBox, which has a number of features that help me manage all email that requires a response. And it does it all automatically so I don't have to think about it.

I also use it whenever I send an email connecting two people from my network. If the intended person does not respond to the other within a few days, I have a mechanism in place for reminding them. This feature alone has saved more relationships and deals than I can count.

CONTACTUALLY: I always used a manual process for staying in touch with my contacts. It involved combining my email contacts and CRM software, and took a lot of time to set up. Then I discovered a phenomenal service called Contactually. It's an email integration tool that allows you to create various buckets for contacts based on how often you should be in touch with them.

To give you an example of how this works, let's say you want to communicate with the members of your group every 14 days. You can create a bucket called "Members." Then, Contactually will cross-check your email correspondence, along with other platforms such as LinkedIn and

Twitter, and send you a reminder email if you have not been in contact with them during this timeframe.

In addition to the members of your group, I suggest putting your clients and prospects in dedicated buckets as well. If there are two groups you want to be sure you're in contact with it's the ones who pay you or might pay you in the very near future.

NEWSLE: Newsle is an excellent new platform that tracks people in the news. When you sign up, it automatically imports your Facebook friends and LinkedIn contacts. You can then import the rest of your relevant contacts, as well as elect to follow CEOs, prospective clients, and anyone else you're interested in but not connected with. When it finds an article about you or any of the people you've designated, you will be notified within minutes or hours of the item's publication.

I have only been using Newsle for a short time, and already the impact has been huge. My clients and others in my network love knowing that I am keeping up with them. I even picked up a new client by congratulating her on an award she won, which led to a longer, more involved conversation.

If you would like to see a more in-depth review of how I use the tools mentioned in this chapter, as well as my updated list of resources, please visit:

WWW.DEREKCOBURN.COM/BOOKTOOLS

ONLINE COMMUNITIES

When you and a couple hundred other people attend the big Chamber of Commerce banquet, there is no way to stay connected to everyone in attendance, let alone start relationships with ideal clients and partners. Even if you're lucky enough to meet a few good people, where you go from there becomes a little murky. That initial spark typically dims into a series of tenuous email exchanges at best. This is one of the main reasons networking is not working.

Additionally, the vast majority of lead generation and networking groups only offer offline meet-ups. Afterward, you're on your own. You can solve this problem by leveraging platforms like Twitter, LinkedIn and Facebook, as we discussed earlier. Wherever the people you have (or want to have) relationships with are spending their online time is where you want to be. This could include any or all of the above.

You should also create a dedicated place online for your group members to easily stay in touch. Having a central place for staying on top of everyone's business and personal lives is vital, and will prove incredibly invaluable in the long run.

There are several great options currently available for this: a community on Google+, a group on LinkedIn or one on Facebook. Poll your members to find out where they already hang out online and create something there. If everyone is already on Facebook, use Facebook. This makes it easy not only for the group to stay in touch, but also for everyone to share and promote the activities of fellow members to their own networks.

Regardless of which platform you use, the main point is to allow everyone to easily stay connected when they are not in the same room together. But before you make your decisions, be sure it provides the following features (at a minimum):

- The ability to schedule and promote events

- Forums for questions/feedback/discussions

- The ability to add blogs and content that is sharable

- The ability to directly contact and connect with one another

Having a unified online presence should be part of the secret sauce that allows your group to maintain connections and derive value from them. Eventually you'll probably want to build a custom site of your own (which is what I did), but for now just put a stake in the ground somewhere. All of the platforms I just mentioned will do the trick.

CHAPTER 08

TRIGGERING ONGOING RECIPROCITY

TRIGGERING ONGOING RECIPROCITY

If you spend all of your time focused on helping everyone else, what's in it for you? Well, to be blunt: A hell of a lot! *If you make it easy for people to help you.*

You've assembled a group of remarkable professionals to whom you regularly have access. You've added a lot of value for them. You've delivered opportunities and deals. You've helped them make more money and connections. Most importantly, you've made their lives better— personally and professionally.

Now, it would be great if some of them were lying awake at night thinking about how they can help you. Chances are that's not the case. They're also probably not carving out 30 minutes on a Friday afternoon to go through their contacts looking for potential introductions. But that's okay. Trust me, they *want* to reciprocate. They just aren't focused on it...yet.

At this stage, the key to adding value for your own business is to take an active role in triggering ongoing reciprocity from your network. If you think that idea means coming right out and asking for referrals, stop thinking. The last thing you want to do is send anyone in your group a cheesy email asking for a referral. Getting referrals was not your main reason for connecting these people, and you'd be undoing a lot of your hard work by making it seem as though it were.

There are, however, a number of perfectly tactful and appropriate ways to position yourself to receive help on an ongoing basis.

THE LOW HANGING FRUIT

If the only way for prospective clients to meet you and learn about your business is to set up a meeting, you're making it too hard for your advocates to introduce you. You have to provide them with triggering events (like I did with my personal trainer). You also have to branch out and create a variety of different opportunities for getting on their radar.

At this point, your best clients and the people in your group should be more than willing to recommend you if someone specifically asks them for a referral to someone who does what you do. Unfortunately, as I talked about earlier, this type of request is rare. Right now, you have a significant number of ideal clients in your market who just don't know you exist. I want you to be able to reach this crowd, and from my own experience, I know your network can make that happen for you.

EMAIL INTRODUCTIONS MADE EASY

At any given point, but especially as your group starts to pick up steam and interact more frequently, someone will offer to make an email introduction. While this person may have the best of intentions, don't hold your breath. You can expect a good long wait to receive this email. We've all been there.

To speed things up, I decided to make it easier for my clients and group members to connect me with their other top advisors via email. I crafted a seamless email template that was essentially plug-and-play. Your busy, powerful contacts will be thankful you've done the work for them by eliminating any uncertainty over how to describe what you do. Based on my experience, you should see an immediate payoff.

In fact, we used this technique recently with our cadre members. All of our members knew that recommending new members was valuable and they were willing to help. We were getting 5-10 high-quality introductions per month, which was pretty good, but we knew the potential for more was there.

One month we sent an email asking them to help us connect with new members, and included an attachment with the email already drafted for them. All they had to do was copy and paste it into their email and send it along. The result? We received over 60 referrals that month! It wasn't that our members liked us more in August than they did in July. It was that we *made it easy for them to help us*.

BLOGS/E-NEWSLETTERS

If you don't already have a blog or email that you send out on a regular basis, start one. Particularly if you have a business in which credibility is a major factor, you will need to establish some credibility over time. I have never come across someone who immediately decided to move their millions over to my firm after meeting me.

Potential clients need more than a free lunch and a smiling face before they trust you. Sharing your knowledge with a list of remarkable professionals on a regular basis can bridge that trust gap and ultimately prompt reciprocation. You'll be reaffirming their trust in you, and putting them in a position to easily pass this trust along to their networks.

> **WARNING:** If you send newsletters[7], you have to be providing information that is useful, relevant, interesting—and not overtly promotional. Clogging up people's inboxes with crap will do more harm than good.

7　If you're interested in creating a blog or newsletter, or you have one that you're not happy with, look no further than my friend Marcus Sheridan, a.k.a. The Sales Lion (www. thesaleslion.com). You'll be in good hands. Not only will having an effective way of sharing useful information make you more referable, but it will also help you attract more relevant and ideal prospective clients from other sources (like Google).

CLIENT APPRECIATION EVENTS

Hosting events is a great way to add value for your existing network. They're also a great way to meet and develop relationships with prospective clients, because they trigger reciprocity.

A few years ago I started hosting wine tasting events on a quarterly basis. During the first year, I generated close to $150,000 of revenue from individuals I met for the first time when they attended one of these tastings. There is no reason you can't do the same.

I knew these gatherings could be a good way for me to meet new people, but my primary reason for setting them up was to do something for my existing clients that I knew they would enjoy. (You knew I was going to say that, right?) I looked at the wine tastings as client appreciation, not marketing, even though they were clearly doing double duty.

I would reserve a private room at an outstanding restaurant. I would serve incredible wine and food. And I would make sure everyone there got introduced. I also asked my clients and strategic partners to bring someone they thought would be good for me to meet. The only requirement: they have to enjoy great wine. I assured them there would be no sales pitch. (You don't have to sell because your clients will do the selling for you.)

I did, however—and this is important—give a brief talk (10-15 minutes) on a relevant financial topic. I did it for three reasons: 1) taking center stage allowed everyone to put a face to the name of the guy who organized the event (me), 2) it was an opportunity to provide some valuable advice for my clients and their guests, and 3) it let me demonstrate my expertise. This model can work regardless of the industry you're in.

Bear in mind, most of the folks who are invited by your clients and networking group will not be there because they want to hire you. In my case, many were perfectly happy with their current financial advisors. That is, until I shared some information or a strategy that resonated with them. Then they wondered why their current advisor had not shared this with them...and why their current advisor had never invited them to a wine tasting.

For me, it became commonplace for at least 50% of my non-clients at these events to reach out in order to learn more about my firm and see if I could help them. Remember, if this does not happen (though I bet it will), your event should still be considered a success. Even if you don't end up with a single new client, your existing clients will have had a nice night out, met some cool new people, and shared the experience with the person they invited—all thanks to you.

PUT YOUR CLIENTS AND COMMUNITY IN THE SPOTLIGHT

Kathy Albarado is the CEO of Helios HR, an outstanding human resource management consulting and recruiting firm. She hosts an annual event known as the Apollo Awards, which honors companies for their outstanding HR programs (and has grown each year since Kathy started it). But check this out: the participating companies are nominated as a result of her asking for recommendations from her clients and professional network.

Via the Apollo Awards, Kathy gives the people in her network the opportunity to do something really great for their clients by encouraging nominations for this well-recognized award. Who wouldn't like to be honored for how well they engage their employees? And of course by hosting this event, all of the attendees get to see how passionate she is about the services Helios provides—which in turn sets Helios apart from other HR firms.

As you might imagine, the Apollo Awards would not be as highly regarded if it were viewed strictly as a business development tool for its host, Helios. An event like this should never appear to be—or *actually* be—a prospecting tactic. That's why Helios approaches their event from a position of collaboration, not competition. They have an independent panel of judges who identify the winners and, to their credit, firms that might be considered competitors of Helios often receive awards.

Could you put together an awards program to honor the types of individuals or companies you want to serve? Just make sure, like Kathy, that you're authentic in your approach and only reward the ones who deserve it.

GETTING CREATIVE

When you are a CONECTOR, the possibilities for creating value for others—and yourself—are endless. I have employed a number of strategies that have served both successfully.

THE 3 FOR 1

In the past if I wanted to put together a golf foursome, or if I had four tickets to a baseball game, I would invite three of my best clients to join me. While my clients enjoyed this and it was a way to deepen my relationships with them, it wasn't very effective for meeting new people.

One day it occurred to me that I should use these events as opportunities to meet some of their friends and clients. So I started inviting just one client, but offering the client the other two tickets as well so they could invite some of *their* friends. It works out like this:

OLD PLAN: Client 1, Client 2 and Client 3

THE 3 FOR 1: Client 1, Prospect 1 and Prospect 2

I told them it would be great if they could invite folks who fit my client profile, but it wasn't a requirement. Once again, that's not what mattered. First and foremost I was providing a fun experience for my top clients, and they ended up enjoying it much more. After all, who would you rather hang out with? Two of your financial advisor's other clients or two of your own clients or buddies?

This scenario, I quickly discovered, is a win for everybody! Your client has a blast (and may even get bonus points for themselves if they invite clients), and you get to meet two new potential clients while providing a great experience for an existing client who can then do all your selling for you by virtue of vouching for your abilities and attentiveness. Even if nothing came from meeting my client's guests, it was still a huge value add. It just happens that, most of the time, spending four hours with someone usually puts you in good shape to earn permission to follow up with them.

If you don't have a system for spending time with your clients in non-business settings, you are missing out on valuable opportunities to deepen these relationships. And now that you know the ancillary benefits that can come from these experiences as well, you have no excuse not to develop a system yourself.

First, identify some of your best clients. Then, if you don't know them already, learn about their interests and passions. From there, take that information and work it into a plan of action. Over time, if you are diligent and selfless, you just might create enough demand for your services that you can choose to work only with clients you have a lot in common with. That's the pinnacle—the mountaintop—when work is never really work, because you're always having fun.

DOUBLE DATING

Don't worry; I'm not pulling out another dating analogy here. "Double dating," in the professional networking sense, is when you involve another professional from your network in an outing. It is basically the same principle as the 3 for 1, but with a twist.

The next time you have four tickets to attend an event, invite a strategic partner (or one of your group members) to join you. Then invite someone else from your network who you think your strategic partner should meet, and have them bring someone they think you should meet.

This arrangement gives you a way to expand your relationship with a business partner, while you also get to connect each other to a remarkable person from your respective networks. You can do this *ad infinitum* with the members of your group and you should encourage them to do the same.

DINNER PARTIES

There is nothing quite like breaking bread with your professional relationships. This is pretty straightforward, but I did not want to leave it out since it has been so valuable for me. You can invite a mix of group members and clients; even experiment with "3 for 1" and "double dating" to pull the group together. It doesn't matter which approach you take as long as you take one of them, because there should be a reason for all these people to be around the same table beyond simply that you asked them to be there.[8] A dinner can be a conduit for valuable new connections all around, so don't squander it.

WHAT NOT TO DO

When you invite clients to bring their friends along to any type of event—golf, dinner party, wine tasting, etc.—make sure you *never follow up directly with the guests of your clients*. This is a huge no-no.

There may be some instances in which contacting a guest feels appropriate based on your conversations, but proceed with caution. Sometimes friendly conversation is just that; it's not an implied request to hear more in a few days or, God forbid, get solicited. You can clarify with your client to gauge their guest's interest, but even then you should avoid asking if you can contact them directly after an event. You risk your client beginning to question your motivations, which is the first step on the path to a

---

8   If you could use some ideas for putting a dinner party together, I encourage you to check out *Host a Dinner Party That Gets Everyone Talking,* a free e-book from Michelle Welsch, founder of Project Exponential.

loss of trust. Plus, there's no way to ask this question of your client without looking bad. What you *can* do is ask your client if their guest had a good time. Then leave it at that. Half the time, they'll know exactly how their guest felt about spending time with you and whether they're interested in reconnecting with you. Just take their lead and follow up appropriately.

Remember, gaining access to your client's connections for prospecting purposes should not, I repeat NOT, be your primary reason for creating these experiences. If showing your clients and their guests a good time happens to trigger reciprocity, and it should, outstanding. But that has to happen organically. It's important to be patient, and keep your focus strictly on adding value for your existing clients and strategic partners.

PARTING THOUGHTS

As our time together comes to an end, I want to thank you for giving me the opportunity to serve you. By now, you should realize that networking effectively does not have to include randomly attending larger events.

Whether you are ready to implement the entire CONECTOR process, or just focus initially on one or two of the strategies, you now have the tools to create this ideal world for yourself and your network. The next time there is an event you would have previously attended, don't. Instead, use that time to implement the strategies in this book. Have a conversation with a client to get a better understanding of her triggering events, or take your best client and two of his friends to a baseball game. The possibilities are endless. All you need to do is apply the time you would have spent at pointless networking events towards adding value for—and sharing incredible experiences with—your clients and their friends.

By focusing on your **Clients**, **Opening doors**, **Nucleating**, effectively using **Events**, fostering **Community** and **Triggering Ongoing Reciprocity**, you'll be able to build an engaged core group of people who do more than network and generate dubious leads.

If you follow the CONECTOR process, you'll be able to create a motivated group of professionals who appreciate the importance of staying connected and helping one another. You will deepen the relationships you have with your best clients, while attracting more of them. However, the biggest benefit to be had from all of this is that as the quality and quantity of your ideal relationships increase, so too will your business and your life.

HOW CAN I HELP YOU?

I am excited that you will now be able to apply your networking efforts in a more meaningful and productive way. This book contains a lot of information, and to help you execute the CONECTOR process, I have created a number of checklists and templates which you can obtain at www. derekcoburn.com/bookresources.

One of the many benefits of leading over 100 CEOs

and business owners via cadre is that we are constantly exposed to new ways to network. I will be sharing what is working (and not working) on my blog at www.derekcoburn. com. I welcome participation, and would love to have you become a part of my extended un-networking community.

As you begin acting on the advice in this book, I am here to help. I would also love to hear what is working for you. Please share your feedback, ideas and questions by emailing me at: dcoburn@derekcoburn.com.

The world needs another CONECTOR like you. What are you waiting for?

ACKNOWLEDGMENTS

Writing this book would not have been possible without the help and support of many more individuals than I can list here. While I'm certain I could fill up a few more pages giving thanks to individuals who lent me a hand throughout this process, I am especially grateful for the following people:

- First and foremost, I want to thank my wife, Melanie, who is my best friend and the most incredible human being I know. As a first time author, I had no idea what I was signing up for. The process was almost two years from start to finish and brought forth every type of emotion in me. She not only tolerated and supported me, but also picked up my slack in the parenting of our amazing boys, Dexter, Caleb and Bodie (our pit bull).

- Yanik Silver for his friendship and for pushing me to begin this journey almost two years ago.

- Chris Brogan for being such a great role model when it comes to connecting people—and for the wonderful foreword he wrote for this book.

- Serena Porter for not only being the best assistant in the entire world, but a pretty awesome friend and person.

- Nils Parker, a master wordsmith, whose edits and advice allowed me to more effectively communicate my thoughts and ideas.

- All my friends who read the early drafts and provided me with ideas and inspiration to push myself harder. Thank you Alan Glazier, Christian Genetski, Ian Altman, Jack Quarles, James Altucher, Jay Greenstein, Jay Sanford, Joe DeNoyior, Kathy Albarado, Raj Bhaskar, Rich Berman, Rohit Bhargava, Scott DiGiammarino, Sonny Goel, and Tim Hughes.

- All of my clients and cadre members who I am constantly learning from, as well as the energy and passion they fuel me with.

- All of the thought leaders and authors who were (and are) a true inspiration to me. In particular, Seth Godin, whose daily blog featured a heavy dose of "Connection Economy" and "Just Ship It" themes (almost as if he was writing directly to me), at a time when I needed it most. Stephen Pressfield, for writing *The War of Art* and *Do the Work*, each of which I listened to repeatedly for six months while driving to and from my office.

- And last but not least, my parents, for always providing me with unconditional love and support.

NETWORKING
IS NOT
WORKING

STOP COLLECTING BUSINESS CARDS AND
START MAKING MEANINGFUL CONNECTIONS

DEREK COBURN